SPEAK LIKE CHURCHILL,
STAND LIKE LINCOLN

Speak Like Churchill, Stand Like Lincoln

21 POWERFUL SECRETS
OF HISTORY'S
GREATEST SPEAKERS

 James C. Humes

THREE RIVERS PRESS • NEW YORK

To Marc Holtzman
A leader who takes his inspiration
from the resolve of Churchill and the
vision of Lincoln

Published by Three Rivers Press, New York, New York.
Member of the Crown Publishing Group, a division of Random House, Inc., New York.
www.randomhouse.com

THREE RIVERS PRESS and the Tugboat design are registered trademarks of Random House, Inc.

Originally published by Prima Publishing, Roseville, California, in 2002.

Printed in the United States of America

Library of Congress Cataloging-in-Publication Data
Humes, James C.
          Speak like Churchill, stand like Lincoln : 21 powerful secrets of history's greatest speakers / James C. Humes.
          p.   cm.
          Includes index.
          1. Public speaking. I. Title.
PN4129.15 .H86   2000
808.5'1—dc21   2002025195
ISBN 0-7615-6351-2

10 9 8 7

First Edition

Contents

Acknowledgments

As the Ryals Professor of Language and Leadership, I would like to thank Mary Jo and Jarvis Ryals for their vision and support in bringing the secrets of leadership communication to the students of the University of Southern Colorado.

I am also indebted to Dr. Rex Fuller, the dean of the Hasan School, for his administrative initiative and ideas.

Of course, without the maneuverings of one of my oldest friends, Dr. H. R. (Dick) Eisenbeis, I would have never come to U.S.C.

Always a generator of new suggestions and ideas was Professor Lia Sissom, ever a source of assistance.

No one could have a more stalwart amanuensis than Carol Prichard Toponce, who helps in solving the everyday hassles of university life.

Outside of the university, I have to give credit to my friend, Elliott Curson, an advertising wizard in Philadelphia, who suggested this book.

Introduction

Leadership is selling. And selling is talking.

The ability of a chief executive to talk for and promote his company is a chief factor in determining the worth of that company in the marketplace. Harold Burson, founder and head of one of the nation's biggest public relations agencies, Burson & Marsteller, commissioned a survey that found that 86 percent of analysts said they "would buy stock based on the CEO's reputation." Burson concluded that it's the winning personality and selling ability of the CEO that is crucial to the growing health of the corporation. If a company's chief executive cannot persuade, convince, and sell the unique strength and future of his company, his company stands in jeopardy.

Burson all but admitted that the services of a public relations firm, such as his own, couldn't, by itself, turn the CEO into a selling star and the premier marketable asset of his company.

Star Power

Public relations people can write speeches for a CEO, they can prepare press kits and press releases, they can devise visual aids, they can make the CEO practice liquid vowels and smooth out his regional accent, they can plant stories in the *Wall Street Journal* or *Forbes*—but they *can't* manufacture a winning public personality.

Today 60 percent of the companies that were on the Fortune 500 list in 1970 no longer exist. The stock value of companies in those days was assessed by the value of the company's real estate, plant facilities, equipment, vehicles, and highway access, as well as by other physical factors. In today's "information revolution," many of the tangible assets valued in the past are no longer relevant; therefore, they no longer count. How do you measure the worth of software? How do you put a finite value on information?

Amid this chaos of change, the selling ability of the chief corporate figure is the key measuring factor. For example, when Steve Jobs went back to Apple, the stock rose 200 percent in a day because he exuded competence and confidence.

Ask yourself this: Do I have the communication skills to rise to the top? Do I have the star power to keep my company growing?

Age of the Personality

If today is a world of change, it is also the age of the personality cult.

The owners of *Time* magazine know this. *People* magazine, which is the offspring of *Time,* now far outsells its parent.

Hollywood knows this. The power of a proven star is what bankrolls and markets many a new movie. The script and story plot are almost irrelevant.

The political world knows this. John Major, prime minister of Britain from 1990 to 1997, suffered a massive defeat when he ran for reelection. Some said his defeat was because his incumbent administration was plagued by sex scandals. Though the sex scandals had nothing to do with him, as leader of the ruling party, he was a lamb led to political slaughter. Why? Because of the personality power of his opponent, a man named Tony Blair.

The *New York Times* reported on February 2, 2001, that Blair is the most popular British prime minister in history—more popular than either Churchill or Thatcher. Yet the article quotes one observer as saying that Blair delivers "a gravity-defying performance of style over substance." The article goes on to state that Blair's performance "is slick talk of accomplishments, not solid accomplishment itself."

Tony Blair is a Powertalk artist. So is his American soul mate, Bill Clinton. Despite the impeachment crisis and the Monica Lewinsky affair (not to mention "Whitewater," "Filegate," and "Travelgate"), Clinton's popularity soared— all because he knew how to project a winning personality.

The nemesis of Presidents Bush and Clinton, Saddam Hussein, survives—impervious to bombings and the U.N. Inspector's demands—and now confronts the son of Bush. Saddam Hussein knows how to wield the cult of personality and play David against the Goliath of the United States.

In the corporate world, as in its political equivalent, leaders like the elder Bush may not survive. Once, when I was drafting remarks for him, President Bush told me, "All speeches are bullshit!" But "bullshit" may be the language of leadership. Bush didn't understand the appeal of Reagan, who had mastered the art of Powertalk.

The Spider and the Lion

The day of the "Spider" CEO—that is, the tireless, dedicated, detail-oriented administrator who painstakingly weaves together the corporate structure and manages it—is over. Those who seemingly possess at least eight arms reaching in various directions are no longer effective. These are the Harold Geneens of AT&T and the John Akers of IBM, who were adequate leaders in an increasingly obsolescent asset-based company.

In this information revolution, it is the Lion rather than the Spider who survives the corporate jungle and climbs to the top of the heap. No wonder a giant motion picture company once made the lion its symbol. The bushy-maned and large-headed lion projects the look of power and roars in a powerful voice.

Leaders with marketable personalities are the winners. Mastering the art of Powertalk can turn the Spider into the Lion.

Franklin Roosevelt was such a Lion. His measures weren't what led us out of the depression. The war did that. But his Powertalk was what lifted American hearts and hopes and won him four elections.

Winston Churchill was another Lion. When Britain stood with its back to the wall, he turned his words into weapons and scared the Nazis, effectively discouraging them from invading Britain. Churchill personified Powertalk.

By reading this book, you'll uncover the secrets of Power leaders, from ancients like Demosthenes to recent public figures like Reagan, from soldiers like Napoleon to holy men like Jesus. You'll find tools and techniques that those leaders developed, polished, and honed as the secret techniques to rise to power.

Not all these men or women were necessarily born to greatness.

- The stature-challenged Napoleon devised a ploy to command presence.
- Lincoln figured out how to rise above his screechy voice and hick accent.

- Churchill developed techniques to overcome his lisp and stutter and make his delivery sparkle like diamonds.
- Martin Luther King, Jr., a black in the white world of America, found a way to be heard.
- Margaret Thatcher, a woman in the men's club of Parliament, overcame a strong gender bias.

Powertalk artists craft talk techniques to enhance their presence and empower their message.

Presence, Poise, and Power

The twenty-one Power Secrets outlined in *Speak Like Churchill, Stand Like Lincoln* reveal the charisma tricks of the greatest communicators and change makers in history. With little effort, you can learn them, too—some in a moment, some in an hour, some in a day. They are almost as simple as buying a new tie or putting on fresh lipstick. Adopting these twenty-one techniques will supply you with the presence, poise, and power to electrify your talk.

Power Pause

I stand in pause where I shall first begin.
—WILLIAM SHAKESPEARE

For most would-be leaders, looks are a prime asset. Yet Benito Juarez, the first democratically elected president of Mexico (the first who wasn't a dictator), was less than five feet tall and ugly. "Poor Juarez looks like a toad," the rich folks said. Juarez was also the first president who was not Spanish but full-blooded Indian.

How could one so ill-favored overcome the prejudices of the property owners, all of whom were Creoles (full-blooded Spaniards)? Or be accepted by the mestizos (those of mixed blood), who looked down on Indian peasants? Yet despite his short stature and the fact that his political speeches in Spanish reflected the coarse accents of his Zapotec Indian language, Juarez rose to the highest position in Mexico.

Generating Audience Anticipation

At age twenty-six, Juarez ran for the Mexican legislature. When the homely little Indian rose to talk, most in his audience were disdainful of him, but Juarez contrived his own kind of presence. He did not speak immediately but looked over the various faces in the audience and forced each condescending listener to meet his gaze. The murmuring of the crowd stilled to a hush as Juarez stood for almost a minute staring his audience up and down while silently repeating his opening lines. Because he knew that many of his listeners might think his command of Spanish inadequate, he used a long pause to heighten their anticipation.

Finally, after that long silence, Benito Juarez began:

Libertad, Dignidad, Humanidad . . .

His compelling words were heard loud and clear by his attentive audience.

Bonaparte's Beginning

Napoleon was another master of the Power Pause. Like Juarez, he was "stature-challenged," and he spoke to his French troops in a voice that bore the crude Italian accent of Corsica, his island birthplace.

But Napoleon, who had few if any peers in the rallying of troops, would stand silent for forty to fifty seconds before beginning his battle address. It seemed as if, for every second he waited, he grew a micrometer taller in his troops' eyes.

Napoleon is among the most dominant of personalities in world history because, among other factors, he knew the keys to charisma. The Power Pause method was his key to magnifying his message.

Stage Silence

Whether you're presenting a new club president, introducing a speaker, making the brief remarks at a ceremonial function, or talking to a chamber of commerce, stage some silence before you speak. Much like an actor might convey a character of stature, you can enhance your credibility through the way you act.

Coriolanus, the title figure in Shakespeare's play of that name, is a man of commanding presence. Another character says of him: "He has eyes that pierce the body armor of a knight." While performing the Coriolanus role onstage, the actor Christopher Plummer registered that trait through a dramatic Power Pause.

> NAPOLEON KNEW THE KEYS TO CHARISMA. THE POWER PAUSE METHOD WAS HIS KEY TO MAGNIFYING HIS MESSAGE.

Try staging the strategic delay the next time you deliver a sales pitch or answer a query put to you during a conversation. If someone in your audience asks you a question, rather than blurting out a quick answer, pause while you absorb the question and put your thoughts into words. Before you speak, frame your reply in your mind—in a sentence with a subject and predicate. A hurried answer suggests that you didn't give the question a full hearing. A deliberate pause before you talk adds weight and wisdom to both your actual answer and your audience's perception of it. You're perceived as having really listened to the questioner instead of rushing in with a stock, or canned, answer.

When you are answering questions, think of the Power Pause as the seat belt you strap on before you drive, as a safety measure to prevent rambling slips. Before you answer, take time to look directly into the eyes of your questioner and hold his or her gaze a beat.

Hitler's Hiatus

Adolf Hitler, whose eloquence was exceeded only by his evil, was a master of the Power Pause. Films show him fussing with his moustache, mopping his forehead, and fidgeting with his notes for five minutes as he faced thousands in Berlin Square. Then, after a long Power Pause that drew his audience's undivided attention, he would open, almost in a whisper:

We want peace.

Amplifying Authority

Elizabeth Cady Stanton, the pioneer in woman's rights, made herself into a brilliant orator—in part by capitalizing on the power of silence. Stanton knew that men regarded any woman who lectured or preached a freak of nature. She was familiar with the barb of England's famous eighteenth-century essayist Dr. Samuel Johnson, who stated:

Sir, a woman preaching is like a dog walking on its hind legs. It is not done well but you are surprised that it's done at all.

Even those of her own sex found the idea of a woman as an authority figure discomfiting. Stanton knew she had to command attention and respect before she uttered a word to her listeners. The Power Pause was her way of amplifying her authority. It worked well for her. Elizabeth Cady Stanton's speech at Seneca Falls, New York, in 1848 remains an enduring masterpiece:

Man cannot fulfill his destiny alone, he cannot redeem his race unaided.

Just as the works of even genius artists Raphael or Rembrandt need proper framing, so too does a speech. A Power Pause is such a frame.

Psychological Equalizer

When five-foot, two-inch Queen Elizabeth II came to Washington in 1991 for a state visit and presented her ceremonial remarks in the Rose Garden, she could barely peer over the lectern that was adjusted to President

Bush's height. A stool was quickly located for her to stand on. Once properly elevated, she paused before she began speaking, in effect forcing the audience to react to her silence.

The Power Pause can be a psychological equalizer for women. In 1957, I witnessed Queen Elizabeth dramatically pause before beginning her remarks at the Governor's Palace in Williamsburg, Virginia. That pause commanded a rapt audience, and the queen presented ceremonial greetings that sounded truly profound. Yet when her remarks appeared in the newspaper the next day, they sounded rather trite. Her Power Pause had ensured her listener's attention and magnified the force of her words.

> JUST AS THE WORKS OF EVEN GENIUS ARTISTS RAPHAEL OR REMBRANDT NEED PROPER FRAMING, SO TOO DOES A SPEECH.

Men as well as women, whether short or tall, can gain stature through strategic silence. In the presidential campaign of 2000, the Power Pause would reinforce the subsequent remarks of not only five-foot, five-inch Gary Bauer, but also of Bill Bradley, who stood a foot taller.

Stand, Stare, and Command Your Audience

Before you speak, try to lock your eyes on each of your soon-to-be listeners. Force yourself before you begin your presentation to say in your own mind each word of your opening sentence. Every second you wait will strengthen the impact of your opening words. Make your Power Pause your silent preparation before any presentation you make.

> MEN AS WELL AS WOMEN, WHETHER SHORT OR TALL, CAN GAIN STATURE THROUGH STRATEGIC SILENCE.

Stand, stare, and command your audience, and they will bend their ears to listen.

2

Power Opener

Look with favor on bold beginnings.
—Virgil

Successful persuaders open their messages powerfully, *not* with little ingratiating words of appreciation or praise. In 1875, a former slave opened his talk to the business establishment of Atlanta. Did Booker T. Washington begin by thanking his hosts for the opportunity to speak? Did he start by thanking his white hosts for extending the invitation to a black man? No! This is how he opened his talk to the southeastern United States Cotton Exposition:

> Gentlemen, one-third of the population of the South is of the Negro race.

By stating that stark fact, he grabbed the attention of his audience. For the rest of the speech they followed intently.

Opening Amenities, Opening Inanities

The prime time of any talk or presentation you give is during your opening words. Everyone in the audience is waiting to see what you look and sound like. Do not waste that psychological edge with trite blather! Go for the Power Opener.

Churchill once said, "Opening amenities are opening inanities." By starting with something pleasant but unoriginal, you'll sound dim and dull. Yet 99 percent of all executives begin their remarks with something like this:

It is a pleasure to speak to Middletown's Kiwanis. I've always had great respect for your civic endeavors in the community . . .

It's banal, boring, and blah!
Now listen to how the great black leader Frederick Douglass opened an address in Ohio on July 4, 1852:

> THE PRIME TIME OF ANY TALK OR PRESENTATION YOU GIVE IS DURING YOUR OPENING WORDS.

Pardon me—why did you ever invite me? I and the people I represent have no reason to celebrate this day.

Certainly not what Douglass's audience expected!

Another example of a strong beginning comes from Churchill, who on May 10, 1940, opened his talk to members of Parliament, most of whom for years had mocked and derided his warnings about Hitler, with this unexpected grave plea:

I speak to you for the first time as Prime Minister in a solemn hour for the life of our country, of our Empire, of our allies and, above all, for the cause of freedom.

In another dramatic statement of reconciliation, Thomas Jefferson began his inaugural address in the U.S. Capitol in 1801 with these words:

We are all Republicans, we are all Federalists.

Jefferson's goal was to bridge the enmities of the two national political factions.

Effective speakers of today emulate history's greatest when they make that opening sentence count. Dr. John Ross, a Presbyterian minister in Pueblo, Colorado, and one of the most commanding preachers I have ever heard, once told me this: "Jamie, if you don't catch their attention in those first moments, the men will be daydreaming about how the Broncos will handle the Raiders, and the women worrying about whether the roast in the oven will be done when they get home."

Begin with a Bang

Begin with an ear-catching line, as did the aging elder statesman Bernard Baruch in his testimony to a commission on the atomic bomb in 1946. He dropped this one:

We are here to make a choice between the quick and the dead.

The Massachusetts patriot Sam Adams opened a talk to his state's assembly in 1776 with this powerful line:

We are on this continent—to the astonishment of the world—three million souls united in one cause.

Or listen to how Senator Daniel Webster began his oration defending the Compromise of 1850:

I speak today not as a Massachusetts man, not as a Northern man, but as an American.

You can also open with a personal anecdote that either tugs at your audience's heartstrings or tickles their funny bones. Lincoln once amused his listeners by beginning his reply to Stephen Douglas with this:

It is true what Mr. Douglas said, that I did run a grocery store and I did sell goods including whiskey. But I remember that in those days that Mr. Douglas was one of my best customers. Many a time have I stood on one side of the counter and sold whiskey to Mr. Douglas on the other side. But the difference is that I have left my side of the counter, but Mr. Douglas still sticks tenaciously to his.

Lincoln knew that, in this series of Illinois debates with Douglas, he had to engage the sympathy and attention of the audience early against the more famous orator and statesman. As the lesser-known politician, Lincoln did not waste that strategic opening moment with insipid pleasantries.

"Yesterday, December 7ᵗʰ . . ."

If you have dramatic news to impart or a startling fact to reveal, try opening with it, as President Roosevelt did in 1941:

> Yesterday, December 7, 1941—a date which will live in infamy—the United States was suddenly and deliberately attacked by the naval and air forces of the Empire of Japan.

Or mark President Truman's stirring opening words from his radio speech on August 6, 1945:

> Sixteen hours ago an American airplane dropped one bomb on Hiroshima . . .

IF YOU HAVE DRAMATIC NEWS TO IMPART OR A STARTLING FACT TO REVEAL, TRY OPENING WITH IT.

Perhaps you are saying to yourself, "Look, I'm not president of the United States. I'm just making a simple presentation of a new product." Even though you're not speaking from the White House to the entire nation, you can still begin with a dramatic statement that's important to your audience.

Crushing a Cliché

I once saw a CEO of a ceramics company open his pitch by waving with two hands a big serving plate that looked as elegant as anything Spode or Lenox made. Suddenly he threw the plate to the floor with all his might. It did not break, but he did shatter the cliché of beginning with platitudes of praise.

Churchill was once asked why he never began a speech with "It gives me a great deal of pleasure . . ." He replied:

> There are only a few things from which I derive great pleasure, and speaking is not one of them.

Churchill believed in grabbing the minds of his audience at the start.

Parenthetical Praise

One CEO said to me, "Jamie, don't I have to say something nice about the people who invited me?"

"No," I told him, "at least not in the beginning when the audience thinks that you are compelled to say it."

Churchill once explained that praise in the beginning of a talk sounds like flattery, whereas the same praise wedged into the middle of the speech comes off as sincerity. He called this delayed appreciation parenthetical praise.

I once heard a woman interject such praise in the middle of her civic talk: "And speaking of leadership, no one exemplifies it more than Mayor Flaherty, who . . ."

I also heard a congressman tuck his expression of appreciation in the middle of his speech, using what sounded like free association to set it up: "By the way, those numbers in the newspaper about costs are as far off as my drive on the eighth hole when I was playing golf with your chairman, Bill Reilly, last year . . ."

Whether it's a few remarks at a dedication ceremony, an in-house pep rally to your sales force, a presentation pitch for a new product, or a formal address, use a Power Opener.

I don't care if every talk you hear begins with remarks such as "It's an honor to speak . . ." Such expressions are simply too trite—like an old coin whose edge has been rubbed so smooth that it no longer has a feel of distinction. Remember, if words of praise in the beginning sound trite, those you are praising cannot treasure your compliments.

If you truly do consider being invited a special honor, say that later in your talk, when it sounds like you really do consider it an honor. Here's an example:

By the way, I have spoken in many towns across the country, but this is the first to which I have been given a key. I only hope that my message can open up new opportunities for your city.

Start with the Strength of a Leader

If you want to sound like a leader, start strongly. Mediocre speakers meander in their opening phrases of pleasantry. The difference between so-so and superb speakers is often this: One begins banally, the other with a bang.

For example, the CEO of a big paper product company started off a winter sales meeting this way:

> We see before us the biggest sales year in our company history [pause . . .] unless we blow it!

Chief Seattle, the great Indian chief of the Northwest, opened his address to a white audience in 1854 with these critical remarks:

> There was a time when our people covered the land as the waves of a wind-ruffled sea covered its shell-paved floor. Now that is a memory, a mournful memory.

One of the greatest preachers in America is Dr. James Forbes of New York. He opened his sermon on man's relationship with God by sounding a tuning fork and then saying: "God hears you and you can hear God."

Fivescore Years Ago . . .

I heard Dr. Martin Luther King in August of 1963 on the steps of the Lincoln Memorial when he spoke to hundreds of thousands. King's opening echoed the words of a martyred president:

> Fivescore years ago, a great American in whose symbolic shadow we stand, signed the Emancipation Proclamation . . .

Attention Grabbers

As you sit down to write your remarks for a coming talk or presentation, spend a lot of time on your opening sentence. Prepare it, polish it, and practice it.

Plan that Power Opener. Then take a Power Pause and deliver a zinger that will zap the ho-hum expectancy of your listeners. A Power Opener is an attention grabber and an audience awakener. Begin your talk with a bang!

3

Power Presence

Clothes, which as it seems, makes thee.
—WILLIAM SHAKESPEARE

General George Washington would freshly powder his wig, brush his waistcoat and blue tunic jacket, and then check his tights and stockings to make sure they were straight. Finally he would buff his black boots before descending the stairs at Mount Vernon to greet his guests.

He was no less attentive to his appearance when he entered his tent headquarters or rode onto the battlefield.

Mien of a Monarch

In American history, probably no one projected more Power Presence than George Washington. It was not his oratory that commanded the awe of those who served him but his aura. Women who danced with him said he was godlike. His charisma was in his looks. At six feet, three-and-a-half inches, he was just about the tallest man anyone in that day had ever seen. He was known to be the tallest Virginian. His carriage—even into his final days—remained ramrod erect. Even the imposing

Charlton Heston, who once played the role of Washington, did not do justice to our first president's presence.

Sir Winston Churchill, in his *History of the English-Speaking People,* writes that it was the "presence" that Washington conveyed that kept the Continental Army in the field despite the defeats and the winter rigors of Valley Forge.

Washington was elected unanimously to be the presiding officer of a quasi-legal rump session that was later to be called the Constitutional Convention. His acceptance of that role gave the convention its sanction. If Washington hadn't agreed to preside over the proceedings, Americans might not have acknowledged its authority.

> CLOTHES MAKE A STATEMENT. THE SELECTION OF GARMENT SHOULD NOT BE CASUAL OR BY CHANCE.

After the constitution was ratified, Washington was elected unanimously by the electoral college, an institution created by the new charter, to be president. He was an "elected king" in all but name. Indeed, some of his Continental Army officers had urged him to be king, an offer he rejected. Even a German principality in Europe inquired of his availability to accept a throne. He spurned that too. (Washington was not the first or the last heroic general to be offered a throne in Europe. The present monarchies in the Netherlands and Sweden owe their origins to foreign generals.) Projecting a majesty far greater than most of the effete offspring of Bourbon or Stuart lines, George Washington was, to borrow Shakespeare's words, "Aye, very much a king." Washington knew how to cultivate that mien of a monarch; he understood Power Presence.

As Reagan did centuries later, Washington viewed the presidency as theater. He made it a traveling show by taking a carriage to cities and towns of the new states. Just outside the city, he would get out of the carriage, brush off his clothes, and buff his boots. Then he would mount Prescott, his white stallion, to stage his procession into the city.

Pop Idol

In a strikingly different way, Benjamin Franklin also knew how to strike a Power Presence. When he arrived in Versailles to become the American minister to France, he wanted to stand out among the bewigged members of King Louis XVI's court, who were garbed in the silk and velvet fashions of the day. Franklin's daughter Sally said, "Poppa, you must buy new clothes if you're going to Versailles."

Franklin answered, "I want to look more like a pioneer than a prince."

So instead of silk, Franklin wore just plain American broadcloth and no wig. He understood "radical chic" two hundred years before the term was coined. At a time when the "natural man" of Rousseau was the philosophical rage, Franklin played the role of the New World "natural man" and inspired a coterie of groupies. He was the first American pop idol exported abroad.

In 1783, at the time the peace treaty that ended the American War for Independence was signed, Benjamin Franklin sported his slightly tattered brown Manchester greatcoat that buttoned from the neck to the knees. Fellow peace commissioner John Adams berated him for wearing such attire on this glorious day for Americans. Franklin replied:

> Adams, I wore this coat on that day of the "Cockpit Trial," prosecuted by that British Attorney General Wedderburn about ten years ago, and I want to give my old brown coat a little revenge.

Clothes make a statement. The selection of garment should not be casual or by chance.

James Monroe, our fifth president and the last of the Virginia dynasty, made a statement with his clothing. He, too, mastered the Power Presence by doing so. In a day when the Regency fashion of trousers had replaced the eighteenth-century tights and stockings as gentlemen's style, Monroe wore his officer's uniform and cockade hat to remind those who attended his levees at the executive mansion of his service in the Revolutionary War, now a distant memory. In fact, he preferred the title Colonel Monroe to that of President Monroe. His garb was a statement to visitors that Monroe, like George Washington, had been a Revolutionary War officer.

The Signature Symbol

Abraham Lincoln is not thought of as a president who nurtured his image. But why did this six-foot, four-inch figure of a man, who towered over his contemporaries, choose a stovepipe hat as his signature symbol? It only accentuated his height. Plus the long shawl he wore draped over the shoulders of his dark suit enhanced the lankiness of his frame.

FDR's cigarette holder, Churchill's cigar, and Stalin's pipe—these were familiar symbols during the World War II era. The statue of Winston Churchill in front of the British embassy has the wartime prime minister holding a cigar in his hand. On the other hand, the recently dedicated Franklin Roosevelt Memorial in Washington is a disservice to our Depression and World War II. President Franklin Roosevelt is shown seated in a wheelchair. Instead of the jaunty, buoyant smile that people of my generation remember from photos and newsreels, Roosevelt's face seems tired and taut. Absent is the cigarette in its holder, which the "politically correct" removed.

The Roosevelt Memorial Committee also chose to reinforce the disability theme by featuring the famous sayings of Roosevelt in braille (but so far up that even basketball player Shaq O'Neal, if blind, could not reach to touch them on tiptoes!). Curiously, FDR's most famous line, "a day that will live in infamy," from his Pearl Har-

bor address, does not appear in the twenty presidential quotations cited on the memorial.

FDR's Invisible Wheelchair

The seniors among us never saw a photograph of Roosevelt in a wheelchair. Roosevelt, who understood Power Presence, never allowed a camera to photograph him in a crippled state.

In 1924, when Roosevelt was to deliver his speech on behalf of Governor Alfred Smith for the Democratic presidential nomination, he arrived at an empty Madison Square Garden early enough to position himself in a chair behind the lectern. Four years before, Democratic Party delegates had witnessed a healthy and robust Roosevelt, whom they chose to be vice presidential nominee on their ticket with Governor Cox of Ohio. There was no way Roosevelt was going to let them see him enter in a wheelchair. When the time came for him to speak, he propelled himself in a leap and grabbed the lectern. During the applause that greeted him, a gasping Roosevelt had time to collect himself from the draining effort. A Power Presence was all-important for Roosevelt.

Power Accessories

Winston Churchill knew the impact of Power Presence. His "power attire" was a navy blue pinstriped three-piece suit with a gold watch chain he had inherited from his father bisecting the vest. He usually chose a blue polka dot tie that brought out the color of his eyes. The cuffs of his white shirt bore gold links with the Marlborough crest. A crisp white handkerchief flared from his lapel pocket.

Churchill, like Roosevelt, was a born actor. He knew the power of his props: the heavy black-rimmed glasses he donned for reading his speech, the cigar he waved with his left hand, and the "vee for victory" sign he flashed from his right hand. Even his hat was distinctive—a hybrid of homburg and bowler, custom made by Locke's of London.

Maggie's Handbag

The second greatest British prime minister of the last century was fanatic about her appearance. For Margaret Thatcher, no week went by without her bouffant coiffure being lightened and touched up. Her tailored suits—either solid violet, navy blue, or forest green—were immaculate and ever adorned with an exquisite brooch pinned to her left lapel. She was a star and played the role. Beside her, her male ministers looked drab. She appointed no female to her cabinet. She liked to be the only woman in a room or in a photograph. With her handbag and carefully modulated voice, she had the presence of a schoolmarm or nanny presiding over her charges, the other British politicians.

CHURCHILL KNEW THE POWER OF HIS PROPS: THE HEAVY BLACK-RIMMED GLASSES HE DONNED FOR READING HIS SPEECH, THE CIGAR HE WAVED WITH HIS LEFT HAND, AND THE "VEE FOR VICTORY" SIGN HE FLASHED.

Her handbag was every bit as much a prop as Churchill's cigar. In fact, one of her handbags recently sold in a charity auction for $150,000. A political opponent once said of her, "Maggie never saw a British institution without hitting it with her handbag."

One minister told of arriving at 10 Downing Street for a cabinet meeting. The prime minister was not there, but her huge handbag was in the middle of the table. No one spoke; the handbag dominated them.

Star Style

If everyone has his or her fifteen minutes of fame, then everyone has that moment when he or she is the star—whether as speaker at a luncheon, presenter of a plaque or an award, presiding chairperson at the annual meeting, or featured honoree at the trade association banquet.

People may no longer speak of their "Sunday suit," but you should have your own "star suit" to properly dress for such an occasion. Unless you are a perfect size 44 long, seek out a tailor. A good tailor can mask any bulges you might have. You might choose a navy blue pinstripe as Churchill did—and perhaps follow his doctrine of selecting not muted but bold stripes that can be seen even in the back row.

You might opt to have a tailor make a nail-head gray worsted such as former secretary of state Cyrus Vance would choose for speaking. Then give your suit its own signature style—perhaps a bow tie or red vest, as a former Wisconsin governor and orator featured. Maybe your characteristic stamp will be a maroon tie with matching kerchief springing from the breast pocket. Senator Margaret Chase Smith, the first woman to be nominated for president, always had a red carnation. First Lady Jacqueline Kennedy wore her characteristic pillbox hat.

> **ADOPT A STYLE THAT SUITS YOU—AND THAT PEOPLE WILL IDENTIFY WITH YOU.**

A CEO named Hamilton had ten ties in the Hamilton plaid. He wore one every time he was the featured speaker, rotating them for freshness.

But avoid experimenting with that signature style in the way Hillary Clinton trotted out new hairdos. Keep your style simple but the same! Think of Barbara Bush and her hallmark white pearls that complemented her white hair. Then adopt a style that suits you—and that people will identify with you.

Sparkle Like a Star

You might think accessories such as shoes and details such as clean fingernails don't warrant much of your attention. Well, your shoes must be shined, your suit must be pressed, and your fingernails must be cleaned. Even a president can't afford to ignore particulars, as this story indicates:

> Abraham Lincoln, who was about to meet some visiting clergy to accept a petition, was shining his shoes when a cabinet minister came into his office for a quick answer to a question. The cabinet secretary asked in surprise, "Mr. President, are you shining your own shoes?"
>
> "Whose shoes would I shine?" replied Lincoln dryly.

The head of a top re-insurance firm told me, "Jamie, no one, no matter how good his background, was ever hired if he had scruffy shoes or dirty fingernails."

Staff and Sporty Attire

A man's or woman's wardrobe should contain staff and sporty attire as well as star clothing.

The staff suit is useful when you're selling a client, pitching a product, making a call, or delivering a market analysis at an in-house conference. You're not a star this time but are playing a supporting role. You shouldn't risk upstaging the boss or department head with overly pretentious dress.

Style for Men

Staff attire is more straightforward than stylish. A two-piece rather than a three-piece suit in gray or navy blue is appropriate; and a muted stripe, but not Mafia wide, is fine. Wear a four-in-hand, not a bow tie. For shoes, don't wear suede, but dark brown or black cordovan.

In addition, invest in what one CEO called "the most underused and understated piece of clothing: the classic white shirt." Treat yourself to at least five white shirts. A button-down is good, but the straight collar (not wide

Italian style) with buttoned cuffs is hard to beat. French cuffs are acceptable if you choose cloth instead of jeweled cuff links.

A blue button-down Oxford is always appropriate, too, but reject the earth colors, which political consultants selected for Vice President Al Gore in an effort to make him more warm and accessible. It didn't work.

Forget, too, the new Regis Philbin look featuring solid green or navy blue shirt with ties in the same hue. You're an executive, not an emcee. Leave the designer handkerchiefs for your evening dress-ups—and your gigs as emcee.

As for sports jackets, wear them at the country club, but not in the corporate suite!

But, you might ask, what about Friday "casual day"? (Of course, in many West Coast cities like Los Angeles, *every* day is casual!) An executive in an old blue chip firm told me after he moved to the Hawaii office, "Jamie, we have instructions never to wear a tie because the clients we call on don't wear ties."

Sporty does not mean sloppy. A polo shirt with khaki slacks and "docksider" shoes, or a navy blue blazer or a jacket with polished loafers, sends a crisp and clean message.

Dressing for success is easy and doesn't have to be expensive. You don't have to be a dandy like Beau Brummel! For everyday wear, try a white shirt, gray suit with suspenders, and dark shoes. I knew one out-of-work would-be executive who got by for six months with a wardrobe consisting of a navy blue suit, wash-and-wear white shirts, black shoes, a blazer, and gray slacks. For weekend wear, he chose khakis with a wash-and-wear blue button-down shirt. That was all he owned. But it was enough to land him a job as counsel to the Senate Foreign Relations Committee.

Style for Women

Women executives have to be more choosy and careful than men do since clothes for women are more complex. There are so many choices of fabrics and styles, and styles constantly change.

For guidance on dressing right, think of what I call the three D's: Princess Diana, Diane Sawyer, and Elizabeth Dole. They choose tailored suits and simple cuts, in solid colors that include pastel hues—but no flowering prints or busy designs. These women look professional.

Accessories to Accentuate

Women's accessories accentuate—such as a gold chain or pearl necklace, *or* a Liberty or Hermes scarf. Jewelry should be minimal. "Rings on your fingers" may be a familiar nursery rhyme, but wearing many rings is not appropriate for your time at work; they become distractions rather than enhancements. And the jangling of bracelets is jarring, to say the least.

As for footwear, take the advice of Princess Diana, who reportedly once told a friend that the biggest fashion error in America was shoes:

> Shoes are too light and the heels too long. . . . The shoes should be the darkest thing on the body.

Yet some women wear white shoes with red or white outfits. Why? It may be patriotic, but it is definitely idiotic. And heels? No one trying to maneuver on three-inch heels can look professional.

If you are receiving an award at a dinner, remember that you are not dressing as Cher, Madonna, and Dolly Parton might be. These fashion disasters show too much cleavage and too little coverage, too much leg and too little common sense. Sure Erin Brockovich made it to the top, but only in Hollywood.

Understating Can Be Empowering

Think of the three D's: Diana, Diane, and Dole. Their classic signature styles prove that the understatement can be empowering. Understatement is the secret of Power Presence.

That advice applies to your scent as well as your suit. Women who reek like "Miss Samples" at Blooming-dale's cosmetic counter seldom make

> **UNDERSTATEMENT IS THE SECRET OF POWER PRESENCE.**

it in the corporate world. Other pariahs in the professional world are women with too much makeup and too much hair.

Because it's difficult if not impossible to overcome a bad first impression, it's best to avoiding making a negative impact.

A woman corporate consultant said this:

> I try for the Estee Lauder look—the kind of bare and blush that suggests no makeup at all. As for hair, "beehives" belong in an apiary, and that stick-up gel look belongs in the zoo with the porcupines.

Remember that less is more and less is best. The "do" on your head should look like you did it yourself. Blood-red talons may get you attention but are likely to turn off your listeners. Your hands are integral to your gestures when you speak, and extremely long or colorful nails will take attention away from your message.

Invite cheers for what you say, not leers for how you look. Women can still be feminine and fashionable without being flirty or flashy.

Be Wise

The reclusive naturalist Henry David Thoreau may have said, "Beware of an enterprise that requires a new suit." But if you seek success in the public eye, your choice of suits should further any enterprise or career in which you are engaged.

Let clothes proclaim your professionalism. Let the all-time great orators, or the three D's, be the models for your Power Presence.

4

Power Point

Speak plain and to the purpose.
—WILLIAM SHAKESPEARE

In the last month of the Eisenhower administration, I was recruited to write a short talk for the president. Eisenhower, who had drafted speeches for General Douglas MacArthur in the Philippines in the 1930s, was no stranger to drafting speeches for others. He even wrote his autobiographical bestseller, *Crusade in Europe,* in 1948 without help of a ghostwriter. I was called to the Oval Office, where Eisenhower sat at his desk. He banged his glasses on the desk and barked out,

"What is your Q.E.D.?"

"Q.E.D., Mr. President?"

"Yes Q.E.D.—Quod Erat Demonstranda. Don't you remember your geometry? What's the bottom line? In one sentence! What is it you want the audience to do when the speech is over? If you do not know that before you start to write the talk, you're wasting your gosh darn time and my time."

Bottom-Line Message

Later, White House speechwriter Fred Fox, a former preacher to whom I taught Sunday School in Williamstown while attending Williams College, told me that Eisenhower had once told him this:

> You ought to be able to put your bottom-line message on the inside of a matchbook—before you ever start at your typewriter.

For any talk or presentation, you must figure out the Power Point first. Whether you are going to a breakfast meeting with a potential investor, making a sales talk, or delivering a product presentation, you need to first come up with the key message you want to leave with your audience.

Figure Out Your Power Point

In 1937, Winston Churchill was going to a small dinner party in a London flat, to which some key members of his Conservative Party were also invited. When his cab arrived at the destination, he didn't get out immediately. Finally, the confused taxi driver said, "We're here, Governor."

> WHETHER YOU ARE GOING TO A BREAKFAST MEETING WITH A POTENTIAL INVESTOR, MAKING A SALES TALK, OR DELIVERING A PRODUCT PRESENTATION, YOU NEED TO FIRST COME UP WITH THE KEY MESSAGE.

"Please wait a moment," replied Churchill. "I'm still going over my 'extemporaneous' remarks." Churchill knew his Power Point: The number of German Luftwaffe planes was a hundred times greater than the R.A.F. plane inventory; therefore, Britain had better start building planes at once. When the cab stopped, Churchill was still mulling over how he might reinforce his Power Point that evening.

He might quote this line from George Washington's farewell address: "The only way to ensure peace is to prepare for war." Or he might want to drop the statistic that if Britain went all-out manufacturing fighter and bomber planes, it would take until 1942 to get where the Germans already were in 1937. Certainly he was going to tell his listeners this story about the Berlin Zoo:

> It seems the zoo featured a cage where a lion and a lamb lived together in peace and harmony. It was a huge drawing card for visitors.
>
> One English tourist asked the zookeeper, "How did you find such a lion?"
>
> "The lion isn't the hard thing," replied the zoo man. "It's the lamb. Every morning we need a new lamb."

That story was intended to describe the predatory Nazis.

The Secret of a Powerful Message

The great orator Cato, when asked the secret of his powerful talks in the Roman Senate, said:

> Find the message first and the words will follow.

Too much of the time we spew out words that are not on track. Harold Macmillan, who would become Britain's prime minister in the 1950s, asked Winston Churchill what he thought of his "maiden address" in the 1925 House of Commons. Churchill harrumphed:

> Harold, when you rose you didn't know what you were going to say, when you were speaking you didn't know what you were saying, and when you finished you didn't know what you had said.

Through this criticism, Churchill emphasized how important it is to zero in on the purpose of your message.

Churchill was contemptuous of speeches that rambled. Because he was a great speaker, he was once asked whether he really enjoyed listening to other speakers at the various banquets he attended, to which he replied,

> There are too many public speeches and too little private thinking.

You need private thinking to figure out your Power Point first. Churchill could easily spot talkers who hadn't yet figured out their Power Point. He said of them:

I can barely conceal my disdain for the desultory.

Benjamin Franklin had the same reaction, which he expressed in this way:

Save us from the orator with his flood of words and drop of reason.

We've all heard and criticized speakers who ramble, yet many of us ramble without hearing or critiquing ourselves.

Stop, Think, and Plan

In kindergarten we were taught to "stop, look, and listen" before we crossed the street. Well, unless you're willing to risk being run down by disinterest and distraction and having your proposal dismissed, first "stop, think, and plan" the Power Point you want to get across. In other words, what is the bottom line of your message? Focus on that first!

> **UNLESS YOU'RE WILLING TO RISK DISINTEREST AND DISTRACTION AND HAVING YOUR PROPOSAL DISMISSED, FIRST "STOP, THINK, AND PLAN" THE POWER POINT.**

Demosthenes, the greatest of Athenian orators, was asked what the three tests of a great speech were. He replied: "Action, action, and action!" He advised would-be speakers to first think what they wanted their audience to do and then build around that action. To reinforce your Power Point, you have to develop it with examples and case stories. But first, work out your Power Point.

Play Your Speech Like a Symphony

Churchill once said that a speech is like a symphony. It may have three movements but must have one dominant melody. Churchill would growl out the central chord of Beethoven's *Fifth Symphony,* "da da da dum." (Incidentally, Churchill was partial to the Fifth because the four notes represented a "V"—Vee for Victory—in Morse Code.) Churchill explained that Beethoven already had that chord drumming in his head before he wrote that symphony.

Communicating with words is much the same. I assisted former president Gerald Ford in writing his memoirs. His original working title was "Straight from the Shoulder," but I suggested these words from the Bible: "A Time to Heal." I then added this support for my suggestion:

> CHURCHILL ONCE SAID THAT A SPEECH IS LIKE A SYMPHONY. IT MAY HAVE THREE MOVEMENTS BUT MUST HAVE ONE DOMINANT MELODY.

> Mr. President, you healed the wounds of war, Watergate, and a feverish economy. Let that be your theme. Your autobiography should be more than just a chronology of events.
>
> Whether you're talking about your experience as an Eagle Scout, a Michigan all-American guard, an officer on that burning destroyer in the Pacific, a freshman congressman, a minority leader, vice president, or president, you want to establish in each chapter, Mr. President, that you were a mediator, a reconciler, and a healer.

"Take Away the Pudding—It Has No Theme"

In November 1999, I was a guest of Winston Churchill at Bucks, an exclusive London club of which Churchill's famous grandfather had also been a member. For dessert I ordered a charlotte russe, a puddinglike concoction. But my host discouraged my choice with these words: "Ah, James, this is where my grandfather sent away the charlotte russe that he ordered by saying: 'Waiter, please take away this pudding. It has no theme.'"

The British prime minister did not like things to be "runny"—whether they be a pudding or presentation.

And the way to prevent that is by cooking it up beforehand. It's too late in the eating later.

In later years, I was to get the same advice in another form. When I served in the Pennsylvania legislature, I took the minister who had opened the morning session with a prayer out for lunch and told him,

> "Pastor, what a fine prayer."
>
> "James, thank you," he replied, "but it wasn't the one I wanted to give."
>
> "What was that?"
>
> "Oh Lord, we thank you for giving us minds and mouths. Please help us keep the two of them connected."

The problem with most talks, presentations, and business conversations is that the would-be communicator didn't first plan his Power Point in his own mind before he prepared his remarks.

I was to benefit from yet another piece of advice in my years as a legislator in the Pennsylvania assembly. Often I would be invited to the Rotary or Kiwanis Club to talk about the session that had just ended. In my talk I would outline the important bills being considered in the assembly—my bill establishing the community college system, the unemployment compensation reform, or the highway legislation. It was a laundry list.

A state senator took me aside and stated:

> Jamie, what is it you want most to be done? Is the community college bill the one you want most? So speak about it. You notice *my* talk is about highways. Because that is my dream—the interstate across Pennsylvania—that "commerce will follow construction." And I then talk about the other bills in the Q and A after the talk. You should do the same—talk enthusiastically about your own community college bill and about the young being tomorrow's future.

I realized that, to be effective, I needed to zero in on a single Power Point rather than present a series of topics.

Chart Your Destination

The Chinese often quote this saying: "Every journey begins with the first step."

Well, your first step is charting the destination you want to reach. What is your goal? To cut costs, expand research, or increase sales? Once you pinpoint your objective, everything you say will be directed toward that result.

> ONCE YOU PINPOINT YOUR OBJECTIVE, EVERYTHING YOU SAY WILL BE DIRECTED TOWARD THAT RESULT.

First, decide *whom* you are trying to reach. A president of Campbell's Soup invited the top chiefs of their respective departments to a luncheon in the executive suite. The head of marketing, the head of sales, the head of public relations, and the chief financial officer were included.

He heard them out on their various ideas to increase profit, and then he told them a story about his own nephew.

> While in Vietnam, a young marine who had been injured dictated a letter to a nurse to be sent to his wife. In the letter he mentioned, "The nurses here are rather a plain lot."
>
> The nurse doing the transcribing interjected, "Don't you think that is a bit unfair?"
>
> "You forget who I'm writing to," said the marine to the nurse.

The CEO who told the story then added, "Well, we must first center on who our primary customers really are."

The great persuader Benjamin Franklin understood the importance of speaking to his audience. He once bought out a bankrupt soap company, which bragged that it "cleaned harder." Franklin knew that women were the ones who bought the soap. He made his new company an overnight success with the line he put on the label: "Franklin's Soap Makes Hands More Feminine." Franklin had figured out that bottom line before he even purchased the company.

"Speak and Purpose Not"

Shakespeare gave essentially the same advice through one of his characters in *Hamlet* who complained of those who "speak and purpose not."

So before you speak, ask yourself this question: What is my purpose in this power breakfast with a potential investor? This pep talk to the sales force? This talk to the chamber of commerce? Make figuring out your "bottom-line purpose" your first priority. Then meditate, formulate, and dictate to yourself that Power Point.

5

Power Brief

A speech that is brief, if good, is good twice over.
—CERVANTES

Ronald Reagan once regaled a group of us with a story about the best sermon he had ever heard. He was a boy in Dixon, Illinois, attending church on what must have been the hottest day of the year. Reagan said:

> Eggs could have been fried on the steps of the Civil War Memorial in the Dixon town square, and the humidity was so thick that you could have ladled it out like soup.
>
> When it came time for the sermon the preacher mounted the steps to the pulpit and faced the congregation. He pointed downward and said, "It's hotter down there," and then descended from the pulpit. That was his sermon!

Less Is More

"Less is more" is an adage that has been identified with architecture and fashion. It's also a speaking technique that presidents as well as preachers exploit as they build a foundation with words.

One of the first things Ronald Reagan did when he moved into the White House was to take the portrait of Calvin Coolidge out of storage and place it front and center on the first floor.

About as much as he hated to spend money, President Coolidge hated to waste words. Reagan admired his forerunner for his laconic style, which had earned Coolidge the moniker "Silent Cal."

Vice President Coolidge had been sworn in as president after Warren Harding suddenly died in 1923. The taciturn Coolidge became a refreshing contrast to the expansive Harding, who once described his own kind of speaking as "bloviating."

Once, after the president had attended church, a reporter had this conversation with Coolidge:

"What was the sermon about, Mr. President?"
  "Sin," answered Coolidge.
"What did he say about it?"
  "He was against it."

Yet another anecdote illustrates the power of Coolidge's brevity:

A woman in a receiving line at the White House once gushed to him, "Mr. President, I bet my husband that I could get you to say more than two words."
  "You lose," was Coolidge's reply.

Of course, it's seldom possible—or desirable—to make your point in just two words, but remember that less is generally better than more.

Truman said that his favorite president was James Polk. When asked why, Truman cited Polk's inaugural address as an example.

In front of the Capitol a thousand waited in March 1845 for a grand oration by the newly inaugurated President Polk. After all, William Henry Harrison four years earlier had taken three hours for his address. Then he took sick and died right afterward.

Some have opined (only partially in jest) that this was why Polk's inaugural was so short. Anyway, Polk spoke for three minutes. In a talk shorn of rhetoric, he laid out exactly what he would do as president: annex Texas, lower tariffs, abolish the National Bank, and settle the Oregon dispute with Great Britain. He did just that in four years and won first place in Harry Truman's history book.

Terse Is Better Than Tedious

Leadership sometimes means surprising your audience. If they are settling into their seats anticipating a twenty- or thirty-minute speech, astonish them by speaking for only five minutes. That is a Power Brief. Terse is far better than tedious! Being short-winded comes off far better than being long-winded.

What is the greatest speech ever delivered? Many say the Gettysburg Address. How long was it? Two minutes. The feature address of the day was given by Edward Everett, considered the top headline speaker of his day. A superb orator, Everett piled up in lecture fees equivalent to $100,000 a year today. Everett's two-hour speech is forgotten, while most of us can recite at least part of Lincoln's by heart.

Brief is also memorable. What speech of Churchill's is most frequently quoted in its entirety? It is his under-a-minute address on the occasion of his return in 1941 to Harrow School, the secondary school that he had attended with "underwhelming" success. Here's the story: The headmaster had wearied his audience by giving an introduction in which he tried to pack in all of Churchill's accomplishments during his forty years in the House of Commons.

When it came time for Churchill to speak, he pointed his finger at the schoolboys, descended the dais, and gave his one-sentence address. Beginning in a whisper, Churchill's growl rose in volume as he said, "Never, never, never, never, never give in—except to dictates of honor and good sense."

> **LONG SPEECHES CAN SEEM LIKE READING A BOOK WITHOUT PUNCTUATION.**

Perhaps Churchill remembered the experience of Lord Balfour, the author of the Balfour Declaration about Israel in 1917. In Houston, Balfour, then the British foreign secretary, also suffered a windy introducer, who concluded with "Lord Balfour will now deliver his address." Balfour opened:

> Ladies and gentlemen, my address is 15 Carlton Gardens, London.

Then he sat down.

At times, brief can say it all. For example:

> At the Other Club in London, new members are initiated by having to deliver an extemporaneous talk on a subject picked randomly from a hat.
>
> When it came time for Churchill to be initiated, the chairman reached into the hat and pulled out a card that had on it a single word: "SEX."
>
> Churchill looked at the card and intoned in measured tones: "Sex . . . [pause] it gives me great pleasure." Then Churchill sat down.

Listening to a long speech can seem like reading a book without punctuation. General Eisenhower, while he was president of Columbia University in 1949, found himself following three previous speakers at a dinner. The others all spoke at considerable length, and the evening threatened to become morning. When Eisenhower was introduced, he said this:

Every speech written or otherwise has to have punctuation.
Tonight I am the punctuation . . . [pause] the period.

Shorter Is Sweeter

Look for that occasion when a Power Brief can trigger the audience's laughter, and then leave on that high triumphant note. Don't dull the impact of leadership by droning on.

In 1938, my father was running for judge in Pennsylvania. His opponent delivered a thirty-minute talk ending with: "And I hope all of you will vote for Charlie Bidelspacher for judge on November 4th.

My father followed. He opened:

> I agree. I hope that all of you will vote for my good friend Charlie Bidelspacher on November 4th, but on November 5th, Election Day, please vote for Sam Humes.

Twenty-five years later I pulled my own Power Brief on my opponent in a Republican primary. The incumbent legislator had been attacking me as a "carpetbagger" who had moved into his legislative district, rented an apartment, and then afterward announced my candidacy against him.

After a fifteen-minute tirade, he ended his address to the Club of Republican Women: "How can you trust this carpetbagger who has no experience and no property?"

I rose, pulled from my pocket a white document, carefully unfolded it to its 18-inch by 18-inch size, and said:

> But I do own property. Here is the deed to Wildwood Cemetery, where four generations of my family now rest, and so, God willing, will a fifth.

Incisive Sounds Decisive

Too many people think that if they are allotted twenty minutes on the program, they are compelled to use every bit of their time—and more. If they expect fifteen, and you give them five, you are displaying singular leadership. You stand out by having the poise and presence to be incisive and decisive.

Franklin Roosevelt knew the power of brevity. His fourth inaugural address took place in January 1945 during the war. His address lasted three minutes, and his message was implicit: Wartime was no time for long orations; we all better get back to work and finish the war.

Franklin Roosevelt was Hubert Humphrey's hero. Humphrey emulated Roosevelt's principles but, unfortunately, not his speech habits. (Humphrey's long-winded talks earned him the nickname of Hubert Horatio Hornblower in some circles.) Once Humphrey rose to speak, he didn't like to sit down. His brilliance, when heard too long, became boring. His wife, Muriel, once told him this:

> Hubert, to be immortal you don't have to be eternal.

Sometimes even a single sentence can convey your Power Point. When General George Washington was elected to preside over the Constitutional Convention, he uttered just one sentence:

> Let us raise a standard to which the wise and honest can repair.

The force of Washington's single sentence etched its impact on note-taker James Madison, whereas the longer speeches of others faded in his memory. Just thirteen words set the tone for the succeeding debates by the delegates.

If your audience is all set for the typical twenty-minute address, astonish them with a one-minute anecdote that encapsulates your message.

Tell a Story, Not a Speech

People not only enjoy hearing stories, they can picture and remember them as well. The head of a company, who was chairing the local United Fund drive, knew this. He was introduced with many fanfares at the Rotary Club weekly luncheon. In previous years the United Fund chairman would speak for twenty minutes explaining the budget outlays and then end with a "fair-share" donation pitch. This chairman began instead with this anecdote:

> Gentlemen: You all see two charts before you. They tell you better than I how much we have to raise and why we have to. But I'd rather talk about a tailor I knew in the upstate where I come from. He came over from the old country, and he and his wife raised three boys and sent them to college.
>
> He called his sons in one day and said, "Boys, Momma and I for forty years have never been away from the city. We want to go back to the old country, and I'm asking you to help pay for it."
>
> The first son, an accountant, replied, "Poppa, I'd like to but I'm strapped right now. Why, we just put in a whole new kitchen."
>
> The next son, a lawyer, answered, "Poppa, I can't. That Chris Craft cabin cruiser we just bought . . . well, there's just no way . . ."
>
> The third son, a doctor, gave his answer: "Poppa, any time but now. Did I tell you and Momma about the condominium we just bought in Florida? We can't afford it right now."
>
> "Boys," said their father sadly, "you know I never could buy a wedding ring for Momma. And then I never even had the fifteen dollars to buy the marriage license."
>
> "Poppa," said the sons all together, "you know what that makes us?"
>
> "And cheap ones too!" said the father.
>
> Well, I know there are no "cheap" ones here in the Rotary today!

The Exceptional Is Often the Unexpected

The exceptional is often doing the unexpected. Advertising executives tell me that the newspaper ad with the most impact is the full page with only one sentence of small print in the center. A whole page is bought but not filled up; only a bit of the space is used. But what impact it delivers!

Don't Eat It All

My wife Dianne has ten rules of housekeeping hygiene and health framed and mounted in our bathroom. I call them "The Decalogue of Diannetics." One rule is this:

You don't have to eat it all!

In other words, just because there is still a half of slice of roast beef and a glob of mashed potatoes left at the end of the meal, don't feel you must wipe the plate clean. She would remind me, "Just because dessert comes with the dinner, you don't have to order it."

Well, whether you're honing your waistline or your message, remember that you don't have to eat all that's given to you.

> **WHETHER YOU'RE HONING YOUR WAISTLINE OR YOUR MESSAGE, REMEMBER THAT YOU DON'T HAVE TO EAT ALL THAT'S GIVEN TO YOU.**

A president of a national appliance company followed this adage as he held the stage at a shareholder's meeting. New branches had been opened, sales were booming, and dividends were up. Each attendee had been given a two-page report of the company's financial state of affairs.

The shareholders settled down in their seats and waited for the president to read for thirty minutes from a text that would include greetings, the usual banalities about quality and excellence, and then an economic review and prognosis. Instead the CEO opened, "Ladies and gentlemen: Our economic analysts today will back up my speech, as you can see by the numbers and projection you have on your sheets." After this he paused, and in a louder voice proclaimed: "GROWTH IS GOOD!"

He then gave a thumbs-up sign and sat down to resounding applause. It is the insecure who feel they must spend every bit of time allotted to them to embellish their record; the self-assured don't have to.

Real leaders don't have to speak long. General Eisenhower, for example, wasted no time with extra words the night before D day.

Storms were battering the windows of the country house where the American-British allied high command staff was assembling. The weather was endangering the prospects of a successful landing the next morning on the beaches of Normandy.

One by one, members of Eisenhower's combined British-American military staff briefed him. One spoke about the chances of the rain stopping. Another reported on the dangers of delay. A third talked on the weather's effect on the landing crafts.

Eisenhower listened intently. When the various experts had finished their presentations, Eisenhower paused and delivered two words: "Let's go!" Again, brief is powerful—as well as memorable.

Short Is Sharper; Brief Is Better

What is a Power Brief? It is the short statement that can be used to replace a speech. Such an abbreviated message is memorable. In fact, brevity is brilliant! And it works whether you are standing before a lectern or sitting at a conference table.

I was once told how a young executive managed to jump over others in his climb to the top through his Power Briefs at staff sessions.

At the monthly meeting presided over by the CEO, company officials would discuss and debate solutions to various problems. This junior executive would let the others, eager to vent their opinions, run on in rambling discourses. He would make a point of listening closely to their ideas and jot brief notes. And then about two-thirds of the way through the session, he would say something like this:

I thought Bob's analysis of the costs was good and Dick made some good points about what our competitors are doing. But doesn't it all come down to market positioning?

His words were by far the fewest. Yet he would effectively summarize the discussion and end with his pointed question. Usually the CEO would ask how he would respond to his own question. He would then reply with succinct recommendations, which he had organized in his mind during the meeting.

You, too, can be brief—by digesting and processing what others say, searching for consensus or a theme that neatly wraps up what most are saying, and then framing the gist of the discussion into one question. Brief is better. Short is sharper.

Exercise the Power Brief and look like a leader.

6

Power Quote

Those who never quote are in return, never quoted.
—BENJAMIN DISRAELI

John Kennedy was the first president to unleash quotations as campaign missiles. Kennedy once said this of Churchill in World War II:

He mobilized the English language and sent it into battle.

Well, you could say of JFK that he marshaled the axioms of the great and arrayed them as artillery. In one October week in 1960, Kennedy paraded the wisdom of Robert Frost and Socrates, Dante and Franklin Roosevelt, Charles Dickens and Rudyard Kipling.

Kennedy cited more quotations in 1960 than the combined total of all previous presidential candidates in history. In the nineteenth century just about the only two luminaries referred to were George Washington before 1860 and then Abraham Lincoln after the Civil War. But Kennedy would cite poets such as T. S. Eliot and Alfred, Lord Tennyson, historians such as Edward Gibbon and Thucydides, and American icons such as Benjamin Franklin and Ralph Waldo Emerson.

Actually, these quotations came not from Kennedy's own readings but from the files of Ted Sorensen, Kennedy's alter ego and chief speechwriter.

Quotes-Master General

I came to the attention of Richard Nixon, when he was the vice president, through my black-ringed notebooks of anecdotes and quotations. At Nixon's funeral in California, I sat next to a former Nixon cabinet member, Winton "Red" Blount. "I don't know your name," Blount said to me, "but I remember President Nixon introducing us by saying, 'Mr. Postmaster-General, here is my Quotes-Master General.'"

DON'T REFER TO ANY AUTHOR WITH WHOM YOU ARE UNFAMILIAR OR UNCOMFORTABLE QUOTING.

The quotations in my files that Nixon liked to cite were those from the pages of history, not literature. He enjoyed reading biographies of statesmen like Edmund Burke, Benjamin Disraeli, Woodrow Wilson, Theodore Roosevelt, and Abraham Lincoln. "Jamie," said Nixon, "I am not going to quote T. S. Eliot like Jack Kennedy did in 1960."

Nixon also would reject a quotation if he was not familiar with the context in which it was framed.

The First Rule: Be Comfortable with the Quote

This is the first rule in Power Quotes: Don't refer to any author with whom you are unfamiliar or uncomfortable quoting.

I learned that lesson the hard way. In a commencement speech I wrote for Vice President Spiro Agnew, I had him end with these words of the French writer Albert Camus.

What makes a job a vocation is the service of truth and the service of freedom.

But when Agnew said the name "Camus," he pronounced it "Came-Us" instead of the French pronunciation "Ca-Moo."

A reporter asked me afterward, "Who is 'Camos'?"

In an effort to hide my embarrassment, I replied, "A Greek philosopher."

The Second Rule: Prominent and Pithy

The second rule, which I call the "General Rule" is this: The name should be recognizable and the quotations brief.

I once heard a Philadelphia city councilman quote an entire paragraph from mega-celebrity basketball player Michael Jordan in a talk to high school kids. After the first minute of Jordan's quotation, the councilman lost the attention of the high schoolers, even though the quote had been uttered by their greatest hero. It had the prominence, but not the pith. (By the way, a poem of more than eight lines won't work either.)

On the other hand, here is a short and telling observation:

> Good communication spells the difference between a leader and a manager.

The previous quote is from Dr. Richard Eisenbeis, a professor of management at the University of Southern Colorado—but who ever heard of Dr. Eisenbeis? Had the same quote been credited to, say, Bill Gates, it would be not only pithy but prominent.

Frame It and Stage It

One exception exists to the "General Rule": If you frame and stage a quote from an unknown, it can be effective.

President Theodore Roosevelt was the first modern U.S. president to understand the secret of public relations

ONE EXCEPTION EXISTS TO THE "GENERAL RULE": IF YOU FRAME AND STAGE A QUOTE FROM AN UNKNOWN, IT CAN BE EFFECTIVE.

and to master the technique of grabbing headlines. It was Roosevelt who changed the name of the Executive Mansion to the White House and built the West Wing to house a bigger staff—some of whom were hired specifically to generate newspaper coverage of Roosevelt. Theodore Roosevelt was the first president to have a media personality, and he exploited it to grand effect.

In 1901, the forty-four-year-old Roosevelt proclaimed a theme for his foreign policy befitting the nation's new status as a world power. Standing before his audience, T. R. paused in mid-speech to take out an envelope from his waistcoat, and then, with his pince-nez spectacles held in place, he focused on the envelope and intoned in his high, choppy voice:

There is an old African saying: "Speak softly and carry a big stick."

In other words, he framed the anonymous quote like a picture and hung it out for everyone to see. He cited a quotation that is still remembered and credited to Theodore Roosevelt a century later.

I once assisted a CEO of a plastics company, who was to speak to his staff about rising costs. In a coffee break he revealed to me that his grandmother had once sent him a hundred pennies for his piggy bank, along with this note:

When you see a lost penny
Put it in your piggy bank
And someday you'll say to yourself
"My, I have a lot to thank."

"Do you have a picture of your Granny?" I asked.

"Yes," he answered with a puzzled look.

"Well, bring it in. Write her message on the back, and then pull it out and read it right before you talk about cutting costs."

The frame-and-read technique worked well for another CEO with whom I worked. He cited a quotation from the biblical prophet Joel at the end of his talk on new plans for the expansion, effectively framing it with these words:

I have with me my family Bible opened to one of my favorite verses from the shepherd and prophet Joel:

"And the old men shall dream dreams and the young men shall have visions."

Speech is theater. So dig up one apt quotation and frame it with props.

Cross-Quotemanship

Earlier I discussed the effectiveness of the unexpected. What could be more unexpected than quoting one's political opponent to support your own ideas? By the way, this is what I call a "cross-quote." Former Republican vice presidential candidate Jack Kemp has a favorite quotation from Democratic president John Kennedy. To stress and stage it in mid-speech, Kemp puts on his half-frame reading glasses, pulls out his wallet, and then extracts from it a three-by-five-inch card. He looks down at the card and then reads it: "President John Kennedy in 1962 said, 'It is a paradoxical truth that tax rates are too high today and tax revenues too low, and the soundest way to raise the revenues in the long run, is to cut the rates now.'"

> SPEECH IS THEATER. SO DIG UP ONE APT QUOTATION AND FRAME IT WITH PROPS.

Cross-quotes enhance credibility. In the 1960 presidential campaign, I amassed a pile of quotations from Democrats like Eleanor Roosevelt, Dean Acheson, and Harry Truman criticizing Senator Kennedy to support the Republican campaign.

In the not-too-distant past, I witnessed one Republican congressman pull from his pocket a newspaper clipping, which he then brandished to the audience. In bold print large enough for them to see, it read:

CLINTON SAYS "DAY OF BIG GOVERNMENT IS OVER!"

The cross-quote again proved its value when I persuaded a CEO to take from his pocket an old clipping from the *New York Times* business section that predicted declining earnings for his company. Then, putting on his "granny" spectacles, he read from it. When he finished, he balled it up and threw it out to the audience.

For years I served on a board with Jean MacArthur, the widow of the World War II general Douglas MacArthur. Every year before the annual board meeting, I would go up to her suite at the Waldorf-Astoria and escort her in her wheelchair into the elevator and then down into our meeting in the same hotel.

A QUOTATION IN THE MIDDLE OF A TALK IS LIKE A BASEBALL PITCHER'S CHANGE OF PACE.

One year the board meeting occurred a couple of days before I was to leave on a trip to Asia on behalf of the U.S. State Department to address the American/Filipino Chamber of Commerce. I persuaded Mrs. MacArthur to write, on the back of an envelope I took from my pocket, lines I would read to my audience in Manila.

In that talk, during which I stressed the virtues of economic initiative and self-reliance, I stopped to put on glasses and said:

> I have a letter from a venerable and gallant lady who
> knows firsthand of the indomitable resolve of the Filipinos.
> Here it is:
> "No greater impression was etched in the General's heart
> than the memory of the courage of the people of the
> Philippines.
> s/g
> Jean MacArthur"

The Manila audience rose in salute to the widow of the American they most admired.

Dramatize to Emphasize

Dramatize and emphasize your quote to make it a Power Quote.

General Eisenhower was given advice by Churchill that helped him turn his quotes into Power Quotes. After the First World War, Eisenhower had become a protégé of Pershing, whom he often quoted. In giving a talk to English and American officers, Eisenhower drew his clear-rimmed, framed glasses from his pocket to read an order from General John Pershing.

Afterward, Churchill told him:

> Ike, you ought to get black-rimmed glasses like I have. Glasses can serve as a prop, just like my cigar.

Quotes can indeed wield power. A speaker who drones on at the same tempo and in the same register of voice may find his listeners' interest waning, but a quotation in the middle of a talk is like a baseball pitcher's change of pace. A quotation arrests the audience's attention. It wakes them up. It energizes them. But remember: Use only one quotation per speech, and dramatize it. Stage it, perform it, act it out! Put power into your quotation!

Start assembling your own arsenal of quotations. Be selective. File away only quotations from those who are famous, whose observations are crisp and memorable, or whose words strike a ringing echo of agreement in your mind.

> FILE AWAY ONLY QUOTATIONS FROM THOSE WHO ARE FAMOUS, WHOSE OBSERVATIONS ARE CRISP AND MEMORABLE, OR WHOSE WORDS STRIKE A RINGING ECHO OF AGREEMENT IN YOUR MIND.

Put them, as I do, in your Rolodex—alphabetically, under topics such as the following:

action	jobs	solution
business	knowledge	team
change	leadership	urgency
decision	money	vision
excellence	necessity	winner
facts	opportunity	youth
government	planning	zero defects
history	question	
idea	research	

Produce, Present, Perform Your Quote

Before your next talk, look over your file and pick the most apt quotation for your talk or presentation, one that will support your data and reinforce your facts. Take the quotation you are going to use, print it on a three-by-five card, reduce it to a calling-card size, and laminate it. Then, in the middle of your talk, pull it out from your wallet or your purse.

Then frame it. If you don't wear glasses for reading, do what I do: Pick out of your lapel pocket black-rimmed glasses with round lenses—just like the ones Churchill used (though mine are plain glass) and put them on before you read your quote. Perform it to make it a true Power Quote.

Here are the twenty most popular "wallet stuffers" for business situations that I have supplied to CEOs for their talks.

1. Winston Churchill [Problem-Solution]
   In critical and baffling situations, it is always best to return to the first principle.

2. Confucius [Problem-Analysis]
   The first rule in being a wise leader is that you must first define the problem.

3. Ralph Waldo Emerson [Facts-Planning]
   A little fact is worth a limbo of dreams.

4. Benjamin Franklin [Negotiation-Problem]
   Necessity never made a good bargain.

5. Justice Oliver Wendell Holmes [New Idea-Change]
   Every now and then a man's mind is stretched by a new idea and
   never shrinks back to its former dimensions.

6. Thomas Jefferson [Problem-Solution]
   Always take hold of things by the smooth handle.

7. John Kennedy [Planning-Solution]
   Our task is not to fix the blame for the past, but to fix the course
   for the future.

8. Abraham Lincoln [Purpose-Planning]
   If we could first know where we are and whither we are going, we
   could better judge what to do and how to do it.

9. William Shakespeare [Opportunity-Initiative]
   There is a tide in the affairs of men which taken at the flood
   leads to fortune.

10. Alfred Lord Tennyson [Change-Challenge]
    The old order changes yielding place to new.

11. Louis Pasteur [Simplicity]
    Do not promote what you can't explain, simplify, and prove early.

12. Aldous Huxley [Planning]
    Dream in a pragmatic way.

13. Abraham Lincoln [Dedication]
    It's not the years in your life that count. It's the life in your years.

14. Charles DeGaulle [Individual]
    History does not teach fatalism. There are moments when the will
    of a few free men open up new roads.

15. George Patton [Planning]
Take calculated risks—that's a lot different from being rash.

16. Winston Churchill [Expediency]
There are two kinds of success—initial and ultimate.

17. Robert Frost [Change]
Ah, when to the heart of men was it ever less than treason to go with the drift of things?

18. Mark Twain [Change]
Loyalty to a petrified opinion never broke a chain or freed a human soul.

19. Winston Churchill [Leadership]
There is a precipice on either side of you—a precipice of caution, a precipice of over-daring.

20. Winston Churchill [Challenge]
No one can make you inferior without your consent.

If one of these wallet stuffers fits your format, then adopt it; make it your own. Emphasize it, enhance it, empower it.

Pick and present a famous Power Quote that will magnify your message.

7

Power Stat

A statistic should tell a story.
—MARGARET THATCHER

In 1990, I sat with former president Ronald Reagan, who was the featured speaker for a dinner address. Reagan ate none of the food served—instead, two chocolate chip cookies were delivered to him in aluminum foil, which he downed with plain hot water. He said, "I learned that from an old preacher friend [Billy Graham] and a singer friend [Frank Sinatra]." The hot water was to loosen the vocal chords (cold water may constrict), and the cookies were for a dose of sugar energy.

Then Reagan carefully put in contact lenses—one to correct nearsighted and the other farsighted vision. In other words, one to read the text before him and the other to look at the audience.

Statistics are like Reagan's two contact lenses. Some statistics are cited precisely and up front to obtain immediate credibility; others are framed more roundly to be remembered by the audience.

When you read a statistic such as "123,411 new customers last year" from a card or notes, you cite that precise

SOME STATISTICS ARE CITED
PRECISELY AND UP FRONT
TO OBTAIN IMMEDIATE
CREDIBILITY; OTHERS ARE
FRAMED MORE ROUNDLY
TO BE REMEMBERED BY
THE AUDIENCE.

statistic to gain immediate credibility. But when you add an explanation such as, "That means we have doubled our sales in a year," you ensure longer range memorability.

A statistic is a numerical abstraction, which is the most difficult abstraction to etch in your listener's memory. The challenge for speakers is presenting the statistic in such a way that the audience can grasp it.

To the Moon and Back

In 1958, the deficit of the United States had ballooned to a billion dollars. For the first time, the U.S. deficit had reached ten figures. The astronomical statistic, however, was only an abstraction for Americans—a statistic that did not engage the senses, a number too enormous to assimilate and absorb.

President Eisenhower, who managed to balance six of his eight budgets, was aghast. His treasury secretary, George Humphrey, warned of a depression that would "curl one's hair" if the hemorrhage of deficit spending was not arrested. Eisenhower was searching for the graphic image of the billion-dollar deficit that would resonate with Americans.

He remarked to speechwriter Kevin McCann, "If you took a billion dollars and put each dollar end to end, would it go to the moon?"

McCann called the Commerce Department and put their statistician to work on the measurements. In a speech weeks later, Eisenhower said this:

> To understand the billion-dollar deficit, imagine taking all the one-dollar bills in a billion and laying them out end to end. Why, it would more than go to the moon and back again!

Too Many Numbers Numb an Audience

In the late 1920s, Eisenhower caught the eye of General Pershing through the lucid prose descriptions of World War I battles he'd written for cemetery memorials for the dead of the Allied Expeditionary Force. One thing General Pershing liked about Major Eisenhower was that he didn't overwhelm his readers with too many statistics in his reports.

> **LISTENERS CAN BE AS SKEPTICAL OF NUMBERS CITED AS THEY ARE OF ADVERTISING CLAIMS.**

It is a lesson that CEOs should take to heart. Too many corporate executives seem to believe as an article of faith that profit and production statistics are proof, much like geometry solutions. Listeners can be as skeptical of numbers as they are of advertising claims.

Rely On or Remember?

When reading off numbers to prove a point, ask yourself what are you seeking: *credibility* at the time of your talk, or *memorability* that will stay in your listeners' minds for at least the next week?

For maximum believability, cite one statistic as you would a Power Quote—by pulling out a three-by-five card, putting on your spectacles, and reading it. For example:

This year's profits are up by 17.2%.

or

Last year witnessed 103,133 new airfare passengers.

or

Some 814,221 employees are settling into new cities and towns after relocating for their jobs last year, according to the *Wall Street Journal.*

Perhaps listeners won't remember the number you read off the card the next day, but they will believe in its accuracy as you recite it. So, to have the best of both worlds, cite the statistic off a card *and* put it into a picture.

For any presentation or talk, you'll be wise to observe what I call the three R's of numbers: Reduce, Round, and Relate.

Reduce Your Statistics

First, *reduce* the number of statistics you cite. Surveys show that one statistic is the most listeners without a pen and notepad can take away with them from a presentation. Rather than citing two statistics to prove the same point, follow Winston Churchill's advice about picking cigars:

Pick the strongest and the finest.

> SURVEYS SHOW THAT ONE STATISTIC IS THE MOST LISTENERS WITHOUT A PEN AND NOTEPAD CAN TAKE AWAY WITH THEM FROM A PRESENTATION.

For example, if you say that "71% of newlyweds cannot put out the capital for a down payment for their first house," don't add that "Only 32% of American families in their twenties purchase their first home."

The use of two statistics confuses and confounds listeners. The impact of the first statistic becomes muddled and muted when you cite the second.

Round Your Statistics

Second, *round* off the statistics you use. The *London Times* on July 5, 2000, included these two lines:

By the end of the year, six out of ten British, including children and pensioners, will have their own mobile phones.

and

[The British] are purchasing 38,000 mobile phones a day.

If the article were to be delivered as a talk, "six of ten" would be remembered a lot better than the statistic about how many phones are purchased each day.

Another example comes from the *Herald Tribune* on that same July 5 about the changing demographics in California. The article rounded statistics when it reported that "three out of four death notices are whites but two out of three birth registries are non-whites (Hispanic and Asian)."

The article later stated that "51.2% of California's population in 2001 will be non-Caucasian." If you were using this statistic in a talk, you would have added "in other words, a little over a half," thus effectively rounding the figure to something both comprehensible and memorable.

The Arabic number system uses the base of ten. Earlier Middle Eastern civilizations, including the Sumerians, used a base of six. The number of digits on our hands, however, proved easier to process. Today we think in terms of ten, so relate some of your figures to our number of fingers.

Rather than say "21.2% choose decaf coffee for breakfast," say "one out of five." We can easily remember three out of four, four out of five, or seven out of ten.

We also more easily remember fractions involving the first ten numerals. We readily grasp one-half, one-third, two-thirds, one-fourth, two-fifths, and so on. So don't say "59.4% of vehicles in Colorado are SUVs." Try just "three out of five" or "three-fifths."

Simple statistics can be presented in the form of pictures for even greater impact. A full-page spread in the *London Times* featured three naked baby girls sitting on a bench, their backs to the camera. From left to right the captions, one above each of the little girls, read:

DOCTOR   AUTHOR   CANCER

That's painting a picture of statistics—an eye-compelling statement that 32.4% of women will die of cancer.

Relate Your Statistics to Your Listeners

The third R is to *relate* a statistic to a story. I once heard an actuary describe the odds of one in a quadrillion. He likened that astronomical figure to one human hair among all the heads of the world.

> SIMPLE STATISTICS CAN BE PRESENTED IN THE FORM OF PICTURES FOR EVEN GREATER IMPACT.

Sometimes all you have to do to find an appropriate statistic is refer to your *New York Times Almanac.* Ralph Nader probably did so when he rallied against big business, saying the entire country of Mozambique has 20 million people with 15 billion GNP, while Morgan Stanley has about the same GNP, with 200 partners instead of 20 million sharing it.

A writer for the *Wall Street Journal* painted the magnitude of Microsoft titan Bill Gates's affluence in this way: If Gates were to pay the same percentage of his wealth to take his spouse to a movie that the average person does, it would cost him $19 million for the film tickets.

Speaking of billionaires, I remember this story that I heard about Andrew Carnegie, the steel baron:

> A man came to him and said, "Mr. Carnegie, you are the richest man in the world. Don't you think you should share some of that?"
>
> "Yes," said Carnegie, surprising the man.
>
> Carnegie then sent a note to his male secretary, who appeared in a few moments with a check for the caller in the amount of 32 cents. That number was derived by taking Carnegie's wealth of hundreds of millions and dividing it by the population of the world.

My father used to tell of his first day in the jurisprudence class of Dean Roscoe Pound at Harvard Law School:

> The eighty-year-old white-maned Pound would stride to the lectern. He then would pause as he looked his class over.
>
> "Will each of you turn to look at the student to your right?"
>
> When they had done so, he would then say, "Now will each of you turn to the student on your left?"
>
> After they had all looked, Pound would intone, "One of those students you just looked at will not be returning to Harvard next year."

He took the statistic of a 32% attrition rate and made his listeners personally experience it.

Chairman and CEO David Kearns used the same technique when he told his luncheon banquet audience this:

> I can see that all the tables seat eight. Well, consider that two of you at each table are going to go back to your office and work to correct the other six's mistakes.
>
> In other words, that's one out of every four in American industry who work just to correct errors.

Compare to the Familiar

Henry Kissinger, the former secretary of state, spoke to the Union League in Philadelphia in 1998. I heard him say this about that troubled area in the Balkans, Kosovo: "Kosovo is about 5,000 square miles—in other words, about the size of Connecticut."

Five thousand square miles is hard for any listener to grasp and process, but Kissinger's audience could easily picture the size of Connecticut. Most had, in fact, driven through the state.

In another situation, I heard Jeff Dewar of Quality Control Internal argue for Zero Defects Goal this way:

If we accept 99.9% perfect as our goal, we'd have to accept these conditions: two unsafe landings a day at Chicago's O'Hare Airport and 15,000 pieces of mail lost by the U.S. Post Office every hour.

Today politicians press their speechwriters to come up with "sound bites"—catchy phrases or facts that are designed to be remembered by listeners.

During his presidential campaign, Vice President Gore skewered Governor Bush on his tax proposal (even though he used egregiously inaccurate statistics) with this line:

What will this tax cut give you? About enough for a working family to buy one can of Coca-Cola.

Senator Phil Gramm once underscored the amount we pay in taxes by saying:

We ought to make May 15th instead of April 15th the deadline for income tax filing—because until May 15th every dollar we make goes to the Federal Government.

That statistic sticks in your mind.

Ken Burns stated in his PBS documentary that 623,000 soldiers were killed in the Civil War. But what is more remembered is that the dead of the Civil War exceeded the lives lost in all other wars the United States has fought: the Revolutionary War, the War of 1812, the Spanish-American War, World War I, World War II, the Korean War, the Vietnam War, and Desert Storm.

Use an Odd Number

Comparative statistics can surprise, even shock listeners. For example, I once heard one speaker at a National Chamber of Commerce meeting say this:

The Lord's Prayer has 66 words, the Ten Commandments 179 words, the Gettysburg Address 282 words. But do you know how many words are in the U.S. government's regulations on the sale of cabbage? 26,911 words!

Listen to that number. If you wanted your audience to remember the gist of that number "26,911," you might say "over 25,000."

A couple of thousand years ago the Roman philosopher Cato the Elder wrote "Why do people better believe more in odd numbers?" The more specific the figures, the more convincing they seem to be.

I can tell a story that demonstrates the power of "odd" numbers.

My friend Philadelphia councilman Thacher Longstreth ran as a Republican for mayor of Philadelphia. He often had to debate Richardson Dilworth, the Democratic mayor.

After his defeat, Longstreth asked Dilworth, "Dick, how did you remember all those statistics in our debates like "crime has gone down 31.2%" or "Philadelphia has landed 8,146 new jobs?"

"Hell, Thach, I just made them up on the spot! Sounded good, didn't they?"

So if you're more interested in having your audience rely on the credibility of your number than remembering the statistic, draw the figure from your pocket and read your statistics, including "26,911 words in the Federal Regulations that tell us how to run our business." Having the exact figure in writing conveys that you've done your research and have the facts at hand without relying on memory.

> **HAVING THE EXACT FIGURE IN WRITING CONVEYS THAT YOU'VE DONE YOUR RESEARCH AND HAVE THE FACTS AT HAND WITHOUT RELYING ON MEMORY.**

Figures Lie and Liars Figure!

Remember Prime Minister Disraeli's comment on the three things he disliked most about speeches.

A problem today's politicians face when they cite numbers as authority is cynicism from the audience. Many listeners believe that the old adage "figures lie and liars figure" contains some truth. Remember that the word "statistics," according to the *Oxford English Dictionary,* comes from the Latin word for politician: *statista.*

If unfavorable statistics about your company appear in the newspaper, or if a questioner cites some seemingly damaging figures, you may want to tell this story:

> Some years ago while driving to Florida, I stopped at a MacDonald's near Myrtle Beach. There I witnessed a nine-year-old boy approach an elderly man in shorts and a sports shirt who was nursing an iced tea.
>
> The boy said, "Hello, Mr. Man, where are you from? We live in Ohio."
>
> The man disgruntledly replied, "I live here."
>
> "That's neat. I'm going to be ten in two weeks. How old are you?"
>
> "I'll be eighty next week."
>
> "That's really neat. My dad told me that for every eighty-year-old man there are seven women."
>
> "Son," the oldster replied, "that's the most meaningless statistic I've ever heard."

There are no doubt many meaningless statistics. But some numbers are noteworthy. Some figures can add force to your point. The right statistics can tell a story that your listeners will believe and remember.

It's all in your presentation. So reduce, round, and relate any statistic you use to make it a true Power Stat.

8

Power Outage

Too many slides make audiences sleepy.
—RICHARD NIXON

Winston Churchill never used visuals. Franklin Roosevelt never put up flowcharts. Ronald Reagan never employed overheads. Leaders know they can't turn their voice over to visuals. You can't yield the lectern to projection equipment, or the power goes out. You can't delegate leadership to slides, or the generator dies.

Yet why do so many top corporate executives make the mistake of demeaning themselves by deferring to their visual aids? Well, one could say that Americans—particularly in the business world—have a naïve faith in anything mechanical. They are suckers for any new gadget or contraption they think will do their work for them. But there is a more basic reason: fear. The fear of getting up before an audience to speak has even top executives avoiding the limelight.

> **LEADERS KNOW THEY CAN'T TURN THEIR VOICE OVER TO VISUALS.**

Oh, they don't admit it. When I visit ranking executives as a communications consultant, they say instead, "Look,

I'm not on any ego trip. I don't care if I don't come off as a big shot. I just want to get the facts across, and the best way to do that is with these slides and graphs." And then they unfailingly add, "You know a picture is proof."

> A SERIES OF PICTURES IS NO SUBSTITUTE FOR THE PERSONAL BELIEFS AND EXPERIENCES OF THE SPEAKER.

My response to them is that a series of pictures is no substitute for the personal beliefs and experiences of the speaker.

Slides: No Substitute for Speaking

For too many executives, showing slides is a substitute for speaking. They don't have to deliver a talk, they just have to "introduce" each slide. And slides are like drugs; speakers are in danger of becoming overdependent on them.

Any talk or presentation should be the oral projection of your personality, experiences, and ideas. Emphasize *oral* projection, not *mechanical* projection. No inanimate screen can match a flesh-and-blood presentation.

A Prop, Not a Crutch

This is a leadership book, not some technical manual; and you, the speaker, must decide whether you want to be a leader or a technician.

If you want to resign yourself to a technician's role, keep on introducing a series of slides. But if you aim to be a leader, let your slides be a prop, not a crutch.

> IF YOU AIM TO BE A LEADER, LET YOUR SLIDES BE A PROP, NOT A CRUTCH.

When I press corporate executives as to why they fill up their presentations with slides, they give two reasons: First they say, "Well, you know the saying, 'A picture is worth a thousand words.'" Then they add, "You ought to see the terrific job our graphics department does in working up our visual aids."

CEOs are fond of their perks—including limos, private washrooms, and access to the best state-of-the-art projectors and slide equipment. They like ordering a visual display to be worked up at the snap of a finger. And just because it's there to use, they overuse it.

Still, the real reason executives become dependent on slides is that slides provide them an escape from the stark challenge of facing an audience. They turn over their responsibility to a machine. My response to the Chinese adage "One picture [may be] worth a thousand words" is another Chinese saying: "The tongue can paint what the eye can't see."

Words are the essence of communication.

Reinforcement Rather Than Replacement

Visual aids should be used to *reinforce, not replace* the speech. The aid should not deflect attention from the actor, nor should it detract from the message. One corporate head of a utility conglomerate effectively used a chart comparing tonnage on trucking, rail, and shipping lines, but he did it this way. He had the chart posted behind the audience at the rear of the room. Then, toward the end of his speech, he strode off the podium to the back of the room. People turned around expectantly, fixing their eyes on the clearly marked chart even before the speaker reached it. Although the red, green, blue, and black colors marking the comparative traffic totals were self-explanatory, the speaker exploited the audience's focusing on the chart as a good way to encapsulate and end his talk.

In contrast, an executive who should have known better staged one of the worst presentations I have ever witnessed. This president of one of the nation's top advertising and public relations agencies used a series of slides as the basis of his talk, but during much of the presentation he had a large television console running videotapes of some of his agency's advertisements. The result was a three-ring circus, where the two side shows—the slides and the videotape—drew attention away from the central performer.

If you use visual aids, project one at a time. When you move to another topic, remove the slide or replace it with a black one so that the audience's attention is not diverted from you.

Keep Slides Simple

Your visual aids should not be so complex that they defy understanding. In fact, at times you can construct very effective ones during your presentation. I once witnessed the president of an oil company achieve this effect in front of an audience. He had put building blocks—the kind kids play with—behind him on the speaker's table, to make his point that profits in the movie and chemical industries had jumped to much higher levels than had those in the oil company. He piled up different-colored blocks, uttering statistics as he did so. The dramatic use of the blocks registered in the eye, and thereby in the mind, how relatively little were the gains for the oil industry. The contrasting pile of blocks was more arresting than any complex graph with various lines zigzagging and crisscrossing up and down.

Another excellent strategy is employed by a friend of mine who is a vice president of a leading national company that creates corporate identities through logos. To sell his services, he carries with him a flannel board that he can prop up on a table or hang on a wall. As he talks, he slaps on familiar and recognizable logos in decal size. The manual action enlivens the presentation by directing the eyes of the audience to each different logo. Had he instead placed a board including all the various logos behind him, it would have distracted the audience.

Now, you might wonder whether my friend was not "introducing" each decal or logo and so violating the advice I gave earlier. The answer is no, because the exhibit was so simple that it needed no explanation. The rule is this: If you have to spend a lot of time explaining the slide or exhibit, don't use it in your talk or presentation.

Most visual aids, unless simple and used sparingly, will kill a speech and deaden the attention of the audience. Remember, not all graphs are graphic nor all posters imposing. Think of a visual aid as a magazine advertisement. If the picture is not self-explanatory and can't be summed up quickly in a simple, catchy tag line, don't trot it out.

> **IF YOU HAVE TO SPEND A LOT OF TIME EXPLAINING THE SLIDE OR EXHIBIT, DON'T USE IT IN YOUR TALK.**

Some years ago I was asked as a communications consultant to speak to a conference of a major oil company at a corporate retreat in Tennessee. Before I addressed the group at 3:30 P.M., a representative of a psychological testing company specializing in corporate management spoke to the 200 people assembled. He had the lights turned off, then paraded a series of complicated graphs that purportedly showed the flow of decision making in the corporate world. After about forty minutes, I heard a peculiar buzz that I first thought was due to a faulty machine projecting the slides. It was actually the snores produced by the combined torpor of after-lunch digestion and tedium of a slide presentation.

Are your visual aids the seasoning that brings out the flavor—or are they the meal itself?

Be a Speaker, Not Just an Introducer

Several years ago, at a meeting held at the Union Club in New York City, I heard a talk on World War I. The speaker had written a fascinating book based on oral reminiscences of veterans. Since I was to introduce him, I had not only read the book but also made a point of engaging him in conversation at the head table. He proved to converse as interestingly as he wrote.

Yet the speech that followed was not a talk, but a series of introductions to slides. "And here is a picture of the tank used at the Battle of the Somme. . . . And here is a picture of General Pershing." In the book, the description of the Battle of the Somme and the characterization of Black Jack Pershing were far more vivid and memorable than the one-dimensional photographs. The speaker had subordinated himself to the slide projector, and his speech became little more than verbal captions for a disjointed series of pictures.

Don't Let Slides Become Your Security Blanket

The problem is that thinking of introductory comments to each slide is easier than preparing a proper presentation using slides for dramatic emphasis. Visual displays should not be your security blanket, but rather a handkerchief to pull out of your sleeve. Otherwise, as speaker you'll come off second best and the slides will be shown to their worst advantage.

> VISUAL DISPLAYS SHOULD NOT BE YOUR SECURITY BLANKET, BUT RATHER A HANDKERCHIEF TO PULL OUT OF YOUR SLEEVE.

You might be surprised how well you do without visuals. A travel agent I know was to promote a Bermuda package tour to an association. When she looked in her briefcase, she realized she had forgotten the photographs of the beach and hotel. She didn't cancel her appointment, though, but worked up notes in her hotel room from what she remembered when she had stayed in Bermuda a few years before. To the association director she waxed poetic about an old pirate cove where couples could rent a boat and drift in the glow of an island sunset. She painted a picture of romantic bike rides with picnic lunches prepared by the hotel. She exulted about the perfect blend of island charm and quaint old English villages. Well, she won her sale even though no one from her agency had ever managed to sell that association a package travel deal before.

She later told me: "It was a great step in my career development—not that I didn't need the picture packet, but I learned the real secret to selling." Her "secret" was in the words she spoke and the personality she projected.

Slides: An Appetizer, Not the Meal

A slide makes a great appetizer or dessert, but not the whole meal. A slide is a piece of stage business that, when used to explain abstract data like statistics or reorganization procedures, is not only helpful but also offers a refreshing change of pace.

Visual aids should be a supplement, not a substitute for speaking. The display shouldn't deflect attention from the speaker, nor should it detract from the message.

An easy acronym, SLIDES, sums up my "do's and don'ts":

Slogan: Make the caption under each slide a slogan, a punch line, or a one-sentence phrase. Don't write an epistle.

Large: Put the print of the slogan in LARGE CAPS.

Illustration: Keep the illustration, picture, or graph simple and uncluttered.

Directional: Don't use a directional stick or pointer. It's too distracting.

Erase: Erase one picture before you move to the next one. Otherwise, it detracts from your talk. If you have a series of slides, place black ones in between.

Speech: Don't read your speech from a series of slide captions. Your audience can read. You are delivering a speech, not a series of introductions to slides.

Great leaders like Churchill and Reagan didn't use slides yet were among the most powerful speakers in history. Don't let slides become a crutch lest you become a professional cripple.

9

Power Wit

Repair thy wit.
—WILLIAM SHAKESPEARE

You may have received advice that you should begin your speech with a joke—or at least include one—to break the ice. You'll notice, though, that the title of this chapter is not "Power Jokes." Instead, it is "Power Wit" because "wit" suggests intelligence as well as humor.

Winston Churchill, Douglas MacArthur, and Martin Luther King never opened their talks with some gag they had heard months before at a country club bar or a local Rotary Club meeting. Yet many a CEO has called me the day before he's to deliver a talk saying, "Humes, I need a joke to begin my talk. You know, something to break the ice. I know you have a storehouse of them."

I refuse. Oh, I do have a massive anecdote file, but I don't believe in tacking jokes on to some speech I didn't draft.

Don't Tack on Jokes

The difference between a joke and humor is the difference between a pornographic picture and a love scene in a good movie. A joke told for its own sake—without much relevance to the speech that follows—insults the audience.

Yet speakers continue to open their speeches with banal amenities, which are then followed by a trite joke. Recently I heard a brokerage executive embarrass himself by beginning this way.

> I'm not much of a speaker, but I know you should begin with a joke. Well there was this guy who went to a psychiatrist . . .

It reminds me of the person Sebastian describes in Shakespeare's *Tempest:* "He's winding up the watch of his wit, and by and by it will strike." Don't hold up a flag saying in effect, "Now's the time for a story, folks." Weave it seamlessly into your talk. Though many executives seem to believe otherwise, there is no eleventh commandment that states, "Thou shalt begin with a joke."

THE DIFFERENCE BETWEEN A JOKE AND HUMOR IS THE DIFFERENCE BETWEEN A PORNOGRAPHIC PICTURE AND A LOVE SCENE IN A GOOD MOVIE.

Aristotle once wrote, "The essence of humor is surprise." If that is so, why attempt to be funny when everyone is expecting it? Instead, sneak an amusing story into the middle of the talk, when it is sure to provide some sort of comic relief.

When you try to break the ice by rehashing a stale joke, you risk plunging into a chilly reception from your audience. Respect is the one thing an executive cannot afford to lose. And you will lose some if you tell a joke that others have heard before or don't find as funny as you do. You forfeit even more if the laughs you get are only perfunctory as if to relieve you of embarrassment.

You won't find any real humor in joke books. Why chance looking foolish? Telling funny stories is *not* a requisite in career advancement.

But true humor, as Franklin Roosevelt, Winston Churchill, and Abraham Lincoln all prove, is the hallmark of the great speaker. As Shakespeare observed, "It makes a speech amble easily." Humor is a change of pace that refreshes.

Chuckles, a Change of Pace

Great speakers often use humor to lighten the mood of their audience. In his 1864 campaign, Abraham Lincoln acknowledged in a talk that he had made some mistakes in the handling of the war. He regaled the audience with this southern Illinois anecdote.

WHEN YOU TRY TO BREAK THE ICE BY REHASHING A STALE JOKE, YOU RISK PLUNGING INTO A CHILLY RECEPTION FROM YOUR AUDIENCE.

This Baptist preacher, in the course of his sermon, asserted that the Savior was the only perfect man who had ever appeared in this world, and that there was no record, in the Bible or elsewhere, of any perfect woman ever having lived on the earth.

Then there came from the rear of the church a mousy woman with a harrowed look and a hesitant voice. She said, "Begging your pardon, I know a perfect woman, Reverend, and I've heard of her every day for the last six years."

"Who is she?" asked the minister.

And the downtrodden woman replied, "My husband's first wife."

In 1940 Franklin Roosevelt was also campaigning for re-election. He shrugged off Republican attacks by telling of a West Virginia mountaineer he had met while running for vice president in 1920.

Now this hillbilly was partial to "white lightning," and his doctor told him that if he kept on drinking it, he'd grow deaf.

"Doc," he answered, "if it's all the same to you, I like what I've been drinkin' better than what I've been hearin'."

Leaders don't begin speeches with stale old jokes, but they do spice up their talks with humorous anecdotes.

The Three R's of Humor

Here is a foolproof way to enliven your talks with humor without falling on your face: Follow the three R's of presenting humor—make it Realistic, make it Relevant, and don't Read it!

Make Stories Realistic and Relevant

Tell stories that are believable. Don't repeat those jokes you heard about a horse walking up to a Texas bar or that one about Jesus and Moses on a golf course.

Anecdotes about the great and famous rate the best. It doesn't matter if your anecdote doesn't trigger gales of laughter because a colorful insight into a historic personality is always entertaining. If, in your talk, you will be discussing different approaches or alternatives, try this one:

> LEADERS DON'T BEGIN SPEECHES WITH STALE OLD JOKES, BUT THEY DO SPICE UP THEIR TALKS WITH HUMOROUS ANECDOTES.

During a tour in Canada, Churchill attended a reception and found himself seated next to a stiff-necked Methodist bishop.

A pretty waitress appeared with a tray of glasses of sherry.

She offered one to Churchill, which he took, and then presented one to the Methodist bishop. The bishop, aghast at being offered alcohol, said, "Young lady, I'd rather commit adultery than take an intoxicating beverage."

Thereupon, Churchill beckoned the girl. "Come back, lassie. I didn't know we were given a choice."

And the story is easily relevant. Almost every talk involves choosing the right course for the future.

But if your company does not wish to change direction or course, this Churchill anecdote is apt.

In 1900, the twenty-six-year-old Churchill, after just being elected to Parliament, made a speaking tour of America. In Washington, he was introduced to a majestically endowed woman from Richmond, Virginia, who prided herself on her devotion to the "lost cause of the Confederacy." Her family were Southern Democrats who had opposed the Republican policy of Reconstruction.

Anxious that Churchill should know her sentiments, she remarked as she gave him her hand, "Mr. Churchill, you see before you a rebel who has not been 'Reconstructed.'"

"Madam," he replied with a deep bow that surveyed her décolletage, "Reconstruction in your case would be blasphemous."

Churchill once observed, "Anecdotes are the toys of history." Since toys are fun to play with, try playing with some anecdotes to liven up your presentations. Maybe your company faces new problems because of a recent law enacted by Congress or some new bureaucratic regulation. You might, for example, recount this story about Benjamin Franklin.

Before our Constitution in the 1780s, the United States was floundering in debt. One day during this period, Franklin entertained Dr. Benjamin Rush and Thomas Jefferson. The conversation turned to determining what was the oldest profession.

Dr. Rush, a physician, said the oldest profession was his. "After all, it was a surgical operation that made Eve out of Adam's rib."

But Jefferson, who built Monticello, said, "No, it was the architect. Surely it was an architect who brought the world out of chaos."

Then Franklin replied, "You're both wrong. It's the politician. After all, who do you think created the chaos?"

I heard a tale of diplomacy recounted by a CEO talking to his stockholders. In admitting his responsibility for misreading the market, he spun off this anecdote:

Just before the turn of the century, the sultan of a Middle East protectorate had an idea to put the newly arriving British minister in his place. He had a tunnel installed in the anteroom next to his throne chamber so the British envoy would have to arrive in the sultan's chamber on his knees.

When the English diplomat arrived at the palace to present his credentials, he took one look at the waist-high tunnel and, instead of going forward on his knees, did it the reverse way. The sultan, sitting on his throne at the other end of the tunnel, saw emerging not a lowered head but another part of the anatomy.

Well, it was not the first time a chief executive got things ass-backward.

It doesn't matter that no famous names are cited. It is a believable historical anecdote that can be applied to illustrate any mistake or misdirection.

Let's move from statesmanship to the sports world for stories. I once heard an executive recount this anecdote involving Tommy Lasorda, former manager of the L.A. Dodgers:

> It is all very well to talk out loud on all the things we could do to make our facilities better. But first we have to look at the basics. It is like the time the veteran Tommy Lasorda was managing the Dodgers in a year when they couldn't hit a ball the size of their hats and so had sunk deep into the National League cellar. One scout in a tank town in Nebraska called and said, "Tommy, I've just stumbled onto a great pitching find. This afternoon the kid pitched a perfect game. Twenty-seven strike-outs in a row! Nobody even touched the ball till a guy hit a foul in the last inning.
>
> "Listen, Boss, the kid's with me right now. Shall I sign him up?"
>
> "No," Lasorda said, "sign up the guy who hit the foul ball . . . we need hitters."

Adopt an Anecdote

The secret to presenting speech humor is to weave it in as part of your own experience. In *Adventures of the Engineer's Thumb*, Sir Arthur Conan Doyle has these words of advice from the master sleuth:

"Experience," says Sherlock Holmes laughing. "Indirectly it may be of value, you know; you only have to put in your own words to gain the reputation of being excellent company for the remainder of your existence."

Holmes is saying that to be a good storyteller, you have to put the experience in your own words.

Abraham Lincoln, Benjamin Franklin, Franklin Roosevelt, and Ronald Reagan were all superb raconteurs and they made their stories part of their own experience—even if secondhand.

When you start by saying "this salesman" or "this psychiatrist," you have already signaled the audience that this is a joke—something that didn't really happen—and you already have lost them. Lead them by the hand into your story by saying, for example: "An old woman in the town I grew up in" or "A lawyer I know once had a client walk in . . ."

> **THE SECRET TO PRESENTING SPEECH HUMOR IS TO WEAVE IT IN AS PART OF YOUR OWN EXPERIENCE.**

When you find a story that fits the purpose of your speech, adopt it. It is now your story, something that happened to you or a friend of yours. Say it aloud, and then close your eyes and tell it in your own words. Once you repeat it a few times in your own style, you begin to believe that it really did happen.

I drafted a speech for the head of a printing company to present to a trade association. It included this story:

Recently business has become almost a dirty word. "Sell" is a four-letter word, and profits spelled p-r-o-f-i-t-s are without honor. But to me the profit motive is not something to condemn but commend.

In that connection I recall a high school reunion I attended not long ago. One alumnus who was remembered as the dimmest in the class returned in a chauffeured Rolls Royce. It seems he had become a fabulously successful president of a gasket company.

Naturally, all of us as his former classmates were curious as to how someone that stupid had made so much money. So after we plied the fellow with lots of drinks, a friend of mine put the question to him: "Just how were you able to put together this gasket operation you run?"

"It was easy," he replied. "I found a manufacturer who could make them at one cent apiece and then I sold them at five cents apiece. And you just can't beat that four percent profit!"

Humor and Poetic License

Actually, the speaker had no such classmate, but he told the story as if he had. Don't worry about stretching the truth. You're not under oath. There is humor license as well as poetic license.

Another executive I know also cited a fictional classmate in this anecdote:

> I remember my high school biology class when Dr. Davidson asked Angela DiMarco, a transfer from a parochial school, "Angela, what part of the human anatomy enlarges to about ten times its normal size during periods of emotion or excitement?"
>
> "I . . . I can't answer that question," the girl stammered as she shyly avoided looking at the teacher.
>
> Then Doctor Davidson called upon a boy sitting next to her. "What is the human organ, Clark?"
>
> Clark correctly answered, "The pupil of the eye."
>
> "Miss DiMarco," said the professor, "your refusal to answer my question makes three things evident. First, you didn't study last night's assignment. Second, you have a dirty mind. And third," concluded the professor, "when you marry you'll be in for a tremendous disappointment."

And then the speaker segued into his point. "Well, if you don't read the lesson of recent market trends, you're going to be in for a big disappointment."

For a story to illustrate the importance of adequate capital for investment, I heard another businessman recount this experience he supposedly had:

> In my younger days I was assigned to a branch office in the Midwest and I remember attending a chamber of commerce dinner honoring their man of the year.
>
> This man was chairman of the board of the bank. His name adorned the biggest office building downtown. He also owned a small plane factory and sat on the board of two Fortune 500 companies.
>
> Members at the head of the table repeatedly recounted the story of how he had walked into the small city thirty years ago with only the suit on his back and all his earthly possessions wrapped in a red bandanna tied to a stick over his shoulder.
>
> As various members of the city gave their speeches in tribute to him, each mentioned the bandanna story.
>
> Well, I was sitting next to a reporter who had just been newly assigned to the city. In fact, neither he nor I had lived in the city long.
>
> Finally the honoree rose to acknowledge the acclaim and thank the city for befriending him.
>
> When he finished, my journalist seatmate rose to ask a question: "Sir, can you tell me what you had wrapped in that bandanna when you walked into this city thirty years ago?"
>
> "I think, son," he said, "I was carrying $100,000 in bonds and another $100,000 in certificates of deposit."

Illustrating with a Parable

Benjamin Franklin also stressed the importance of investment with a story. Note how he incorporated this parable of what happened to the merchant into his own experience.

> Now this shoemaker I knew in Philadelphia was soon to be off by coach to New York to visit his brother. So he needed to find a stable where he could keep his horse.

He went to the first livery and the owner said, "We charge twenty dollars a month for the feeding and watering of your horse, but we give you back two dollars for our use of the manure."

"Twenty dollars! Good heavens, that's ridiculous," said the cobbler, and he left to look elsewhere.

At another stable, the liveryman gave his cost: "It's ten dollars a month, but we give you back a dollar for the manure."

The shoemaker shook his head and asked if the liveryman knew someone who would charge less.

"Well," the liveryman answered, "there's an old Quaker off Arch Street with fees of only five dollars a month."

So the shoemaker inquired at the Quaker's.

"Yes," the Quaker said, "I charge only five dollars a month for keeping your horse."

"What about the manure?" asked the cobbler.

"Manure? At five dollars a month there will be no manure!"

Here's my favorite "realistic" story that I've incorporated into speech drafts for several corporate clients.

Some weeks ago I ran into an old friend at a restaurant and asked him how his daughter, Jennifer, was doing at the state university.

He shook his head and handed me this letter that he had in the inside pocket of his jacket. I read it and asked him if I could have a copy of it. I have it right with me. [Here the speaker pulls out a folded, signed, typed letter from his pocket and reads:]

Dear Mom and Dad,

I won't be coming home for Christmas. I'm leaving college and moving to Nepal. I'm also pregnant and my boyfriend is a Buddhist. I'm moving to his home on the top of a Himalayan mountain.

Love,
Jenny

P.S. I'm not pregnant. I'm not becoming a Buddhist. I'm not moving to Nepal. But I did fail calculus and biology. But it does put those grades more in perspective.

See you at Christmas,
Jenny

The relevance of this college letter story works any time any executive discusses a few recent problems but wants to put them in the perspective of the larger picture.

Right, you're saying to yourself, it's *relevant* and *realistic.* But what about the third R, which is *don't read it?*

Tell Rather Than Read a Funny Story

Tell as though from your own experience rather than read a humorous anecdote or story from your speech text. The only exception to the "don't read" rule is when something that's written serves as a prop for the story, such as the college letter or perhaps a newspaper clipping referred to in an anecdote.

> TELL AS THOUGH FROM YOUR OWN EXPERIENCE RATHER THAN READ A HUMOROUS ANECDOTE OR STORY FROM YOUR SPEECH TEXT.

If the anecdote comes in the middle of a talk, put it in a bracket [the Churchill anecdote], or [the 4% profit story], or the [Benjamin Franklin "chaos" tale].

That's how Franklin Roosevelt and Ronald Reagan did it. Of course, they had told the stories they used often enough that they knew them by heart.

Reagan, for example, used to regale audiences with this Churchill story:

Sir Winston Churchill was invited by the British Women's Temperance Union to deliver an address at the Savoy Hotel in 1953.

In her introduction of the seventy-eight-year-old prime minister, the Temperance Chairperson said, "You know, Sir Winston, our organization, while it admires your statesmanship, does not approve of your bibulous habits.

"As a matter of fact, we have estimated that if all the wine, whiskey, and brandy you have consumed in your life was poured into this ballroom, it would come right up to your chin."

In answer, Churchill said, "Madame President, I accept the accuracy of your calculations. But as I look at the high ceiling of this room and ponder my seventy-eight years, my only thought is this: How much left to do and how little time to do it!"

But on Reagan's five by five card, the story looked like this:

Churchill
Women's Temperance Union
chairman's calculation—of alcohol
If poured into room
up to chin
Churchill—high ceiling—age
"HOW MUCH LEFT TO DO—HOW LITTLE TIME TO DO IT.

For an executive who served in World War II, I drafted this story:

I went back to Normandy with a group of veterans, and one guy I met told me of his experience just before D day.

In those days before the Normandy invasion, trains were very crowded because of the thousands of troops stationed in Britain. A young G.I. who had been up all night boarded the train in Bristol in the south of England. He entered a compartment where five people and one dog were seated in the six-seat cubicle. Approaching the lady who was the owner of the little Pekinese, he said, "Ma'am, may I sit down?"

"Absolutely not," replied the dog owner.

After fifteen minutes of standing, the tired GI again asked, "Ma'am, if you don't mind, I have been standing up all night. I love dogs and I could hold it on my lap."

"Indeed not," said the lady.

Thirty minutes later the GI said, "I've been standing for forty-five minutes. I have twenty-four hours of leave. Would you please let me sit down for a minute?"

"Young man, you are absolutely impertinent," she said as she hugged her little Pekinese.

At that, the soldier opened up the window, grasped the Pekinese, threw it out the window, and sat down.

Then a mustachioed brigadier sitting across from them said, "You know, that's the trouble with you Americans—you always do things the wrong way. You drive on the wrong side of the street, you hold your fork with the wrong hand, and now you throw out the wrong bitch."

For that story, his five-by-eight card included these notes:

Pvt.—seat crowded train
Fat lady with Peke
Refuses—"Absolutely Not"
2nd Time—you Americans rude
Third time refused
Put dog out window
Brigadier—opposite
"drive wrong side of road"
"fork wrong hand"
"THROW OUT THE WRONG BITCH"

If you try to read a humorous story word by word, you'll die at the podium. Before you give your talk, practice telling it aloud a few times, then reduce it to a few brief phrases to jog your memory. Look at the card to refresh your memory, and tell it while you're looking at the audience, not looking down at your notes.

At the beginning of this chapter, I wrote that starting a talk or presentation with a joke is a no-no.

After all, I explained, Churchill didn't begin a speech with some yarn or gag. But Churchill would have done so *if* the comic illustration had been the whole thrust of a very short talk. Churchill once rose to attack appeasement. He began this way:

> When I was a boy, I used to look forward to the London arrival of the Barnum and Bailey Circus. But there was one show that my nanny would not let me see. She said, "Winston, it is too revolting a spectacle for the human eye."
>
> The sideshow was called "The Boneless Wonder." Now, after thirty-six years, where do I finally find this freak?
>
> Not in the circus, but here in the House of Commons, sitting on the front bench are the boneless wonders.

> **IF YOU TRY TO READ A HUMOROUS STORY WORD BY WORD, YOU'LL DIE AT THE PODIUM.**

That is how Churchill characterized the spineless appeasement of the prime minister and foreign secretary toward Hitler.

The introduction of a speaker might include humor. For example, I once introduced a New York lawyer this way.

> Our speaker today is qualified by both background and experience. In no way is he like my nephew George. That boy barely managed to get up sufficient courage to show his report card to his father and ask for his signature. When my brother saw George's grades, a D and an F, he berated my nephew for such a poor record. When the reprimand was over, George asked my brother, "Dad, do you think it is because of heredity or environment?"
>
> Well, a Phi Beta Kappa from Princeton and litigation head of one of Manhattan's most prestigious law firms must have had brainy parents as well as years of trial experience.

The head of a food company, when presenting an award to the salesman of the year, began with this Lincoln anecdote:

> In 1864, General Grant was one of the few Union generals engaging the enemy, winning victories, and advancing southward.

One day Secretary of War Edwin Stanton brought in a confidential report to President Lincoln.

"Mr. President," said the bearded Stanton, "these papers document witnesses who have observed General Grant actually imbibing in his tent."

"Is that so?" drawled Lincoln. "Does the report also reveal the brand of whiskey he was drinking?"

"I don't understand why that is necessary," said the confused Secretary Stanton.

"Because," answered Lincoln, "I want to send a case of it to my other generals."

Well, I would like to know whether our friend Dick Standish here eats Cheerios or Wheaties for breakfast, and whether Dewar's or Johnnie Walker is his favorite poison.

Because I'd send some to the rest of you.

Ending or Beginning with Humor

The humorous story can be the way to launch a brief two-minute talk and can also be an effective way to end a talk.

At the Sunday breakfast of a weekend trade association conference, the association head gave these closing remarks:

I want to say thanks for the last few days. I got some knowledge and some fun out of it. It reminds me of a fur store merchant I met recently in Philadelphia when I was looking for an anniversary gift for my wife. When I walked into the store, one of the managers was giving a bum's rush to get some guy out of the store. Later, I heard the furrier tell what happened. It seems this young man and a blonde companion came into the store on the previous Friday afternoon. The man told the clerk that he wanted to look at the most expensive fur coat in the place. The clerk was doubtful so brought out a nice squirrel-skin job.

"Take it away," said the customer. "Apparently, you didn't hear what I said. I want the most expensive coat you have."

So the clerk trotted out a beaver coat. Then a sealskin, then a sheared raccoon, but each time with the same result. So finally the clerk shot the works and brought out a $5,000 mutation mink.

When the man saw that, his eyes lit up. Turning to the blonde, he said, "That's the idea. Try it on and see how it looks." And to the clerk, "I want to charge it. Go ahead and check my credit. Sew the name 'Bunni' on the back of the coat. I'll be back on Monday to pick it up."

"Certainly, sir, anything you say," the clerk responded.

Well, on Monday the young man who'd bought the fur coat arrived at the store alone. The minute he walked in, the clerk rushed up to him shaking his fist, followed by the floorwalker, the chief buyer, the manager, and the credit manager. All were shouting at him. "We've looked you up," said the angry credit manager. "You have no more credit than a mouse. You couldn't charge a toothbrush."

"Now calm yourself," said the man. "I haven't taken anything out of your store. I just came in to thank you for a wonderful weekend."

Another time I was present when, at the end of the dinner, an executive hoisted his wine glass, expressed thanks to the host, and told this Churchill story.

I think we all are grateful to our host for this splendid repast. It is certainly far superior to the one Winston Churchill had at the home of the duke and duchess of Westminster.

A friend asked Churchill when he returned to London the next Monday how the Saturday dinner had gone. Churchill replied, "If the champagne had been as dry as the cigars, if the Chardonnay had been as cold as the soup, if the beef had been as rare as the service, if the brandy had been as old as the chicken, if the chicken's breast had been as plump as the maid's, and if the maid had been as willing as the duchess, it would have been a splendid evening!"

So wield wit like Churchill. Be a raconteur like Reagan. Make your anecdotes realistic and relevant, and be sure you tell it in your own words rather than memorize or read it! Glance quickly at your notes to jog your memory if necessary. Remember that the secret of humor, as Reagan once said, is to be entertaining while enlightening, and vice versa.

Power Parable

Through parables of sunlight.
—DYLAN THOMAS

Jesus Christ never used the word "salvation." It was Paul who used the Greek word in his letters, for he wrote his epistles in the Greek language. Instead, Jesus preached about a young man who blew his wad on wine, women, and song, then came back and said, "Dad, forgive me and let me have a second chance." That is "salvation" expressed in a story.

Do you think those illiterate shepherds and fishermen would have understood "salvation"? It would be like using the word "synergy" while speaking to a bunch of cowboys about the combined effect of roping and branding on the ranch. People cannot picture words like "salvation" or "synergy."

Years after the death of Jesus, his disciples remembered his sermons and delivered their recollections when the New Testament was being written. Why? Because Jesus spun parables to explain abstract virtues.

Parables Provide Pictures of Abstractions

"Humanity" is another such abstraction. For that Jesus described how a beaten-up guy on the side of a road who looked like what we would call a "homeless" was passed by several Jews. But then a Samaritan—not a Jew, but one of another tribe—was the one who stopped by to administer to him. "Humanity" in this story is personified in the Good Samaritan, now a widely used term for people who help others. Parables give pictures to abstractions.

Most of Jesus's teaching was through parables like the parable of the tower or the parable of the mustard seed. The Bible even includes one about investment, the parable of the talent.

Remember the story of the man who leaves some of his savings (silver coins, called "talents") with his employee when he goes off on a trip? Later, when the master returns and asks about his money, the employee goes out back to dig up the coins he had hidden for his master.

And the boss fires the employee ("Oh sluggish servant . . .") for not investing the money, but instead letting it rot in the ground.

"Don't Change Horses in the Middle of the Stream"

The power of a parable is well illustrated with this story about President Abraham Lincoln, who looked like a sure loser for re-election in 1864.

> "EXPERIENCE" IS AN ABSTRACT WORD, INEFFECTIVE WITHOUT ANY PICTURE TO MAKE THE ASSET SINK INTO THE MINDS OF THE PUBLIC.

Republican politicians thought so anyway. Congressman Thaddeus Stevens of Pennsylvania turned down an invitation to be on the platform in Gettysburg with Lincoln, a town where Stevens kept a law office. Stevens actually smirked, "Let the dead bury the dead."

Meanwhile, Lincoln's best asset for winning was his experience as the incumbent president. But to say "I have experience . . ." wouldn't work. "Experience" is an abstract word, ineffective without any picture to make the asset sink into the minds of the public.

So Lincoln instead regaled his audience with the story of the Illinois farmer who wouldn't change horses in the middle of the stream.

That single story rallied rural America behind him, and Lincoln won the election. And again, the power of a parable resulted in a commonly used and understood phrase.

Turn Concepts into Concrete

Churchill, in his "Scaffolding of Rhetoric" notes, said that an abstract idea goes in one ear and out the other—never establishing itself unless it is reinforced by a picture or story. Turn concepts into concrete if you want them to be understood and remembered. That's what Churchill was doing when he told the story of the "Boneless Wonder" (see page 83), relating it to spineless politicians.

> TURN CONCEPTS INTO CONCRETE IF YOU WANT THEM TO BE UNDERSTOOD AND REMEMBERED.

A business acquaintance of mine, head of a start-up company, turned his concept into concrete when he met with prospective investors at a breakfast at Four Seasons in Philadelphia. While arguing for double the investment capital his prospective investors had suggested, my friend told this tale of a former colleague who had retired:

Well, I want to tell you about Bob, a friend of mine who took early retirement. Now he and his wife Marge always had this idea of retiring to this little town in Maine (his wife's people were "Down-Easters") and owning a general store.

After a few years they went belly up. It seems that a general store in Maine needed to have everything including the kitchen sink—pots, pans, cots, garbage cans, boots, shirts, flashlights, playing cards, and God knows what else. And yet the stuff didn't move. They hadn't figured enough for the original outlay and they went bust. It's the old story of insufficient capital.

His story hit home, and the investors agreed to double their proposed outlay.

Arsenal of Anecdotes

Benjamin Franklin was no speechmaker like some of our Founding Fathers, but he had an arsenal of anecdotes with which to press home any point.

Perhaps the first American to be the equivalent of the self-made millionaire, he introduced to the business world the modern innovations of mail catalogues, franchising, and money-back guarantees. He was a born salesman who successfully used his skill not only to enrich himself but to help secure our country's independence from England.

Without his talents of persuasion King Louis might not have lent the money to keep George Washington's Continental Army in the field. The Declaration of Independence might not have been ratified, and the Constitution might not have been written. As one story goes:

> When Franklin was our minister to France he attended a fancy ball in Versailles. He spotted King Louis XVI across the room. In his conversation with the French monarch, he pointed out a "thin mademoiselle." Although he knew that the king's fancied the more voluptuous types, Franklin said, "Sire, there's a pretty girl."
>
> The king demurred, "Ah, Franklin, it's a pity that God did not endow her, for she does no justice to her décolletage."
>
> "True, Sire, but you can endow us because our country has the same problem as the young lady—an uncovered deficit."
>
> The king laughed, and Franklin got the loan.

Franklin's arsenal included an anecdote that he told when the French prime minister, Count Vergennes, questioned the resolve of the Americans to keep fighting the uphill struggle against the overwhelming forces of the British army:

> A French priest and Huguenot pastor once had an argument about predestination.
>
> The priest argued, "Monsieur, do you really believe in pre-judgment?"
>
> The Calvinist preacher nodded assent.
>
> "I mean, Monsieur, do you really subscribe to the tenets of foreordainment?"
>
> "*Oui,*" the minister replied.
>
> "You agree with the doctrine of predestination?"
>
> "Well," said the preacher, "I'd rather be a Calvinist knowing I'm going to Hell than a Catholic not knowing where the Hell I'm going."
>
> You see, Count Vergennes, we're ready to go through Hell to find our fate, which is as freedom.

Storehouse of Stories

I met a "Million Dollar Round Table" insurance executive at one of the speeches I give on communication selling. He told me this:

> Jamie, I didn't go to college, I could not tell you the law cases on things like contributory negligence that gave companies all the loopholes on the coverage, and I cannot cite the policy clauses from the top of my head, but I surely can scare the wits out of those I call on with might happen if they are not insured.
>
> I've collected, Jamie, what I call my "terrible tales"—real-life horror stories of those who didn't have insurance, stories that would curl your hair. I have everything from crying widows to homeless orphans—all because there was no insurance.
>
> I had a three-by-five card file on every sob story or funny tale that I had ever read about or heard in reference to not carrying insurance. Some would bring tears, others laughter.

And Jamie, most of the time it worked, I sold the policy. And you know, my son-in-law is now in the business. As I told him, "All you need is a story a day to sell."

I've found parables so valuable that I've collected dozens that will fit almost any occasion or topic. What originally brought me to the attention of the White House was not my craft as a wordsmith but my collection of historical anecdotes. In fact, William Safire, in his book *Before the Fall*, quotes Nixon as saying, "Why can't you come up with the parables like Jamie Humes?"

Once President Nixon had to deliver some short remarks on the retirement of a Cabinet member and asked me for help. I sent Nixon this story:

> When Thomas Jefferson arrived to present his credentials to be minister to France, the French prime minister said, "Monsieur Jefferson, have you come to replace Dr. Franklin?"
>
> "No, Your Excellency," replied Jefferson. "No one could ever replace Dr. Franklin. I am only succeeding him."

The plus side of this particular parable is that it was easy to memorize. Nixon didn't have to read his remarks the next day. He just had to remember Franklin and Jefferson and the key words "succeed" and "replace."

For the rest of his remarks, Nixon would say, "And no one could ever replace the secretary's experience, knowledge, or commitment to public service."

LOOK BACK ON YOUR OWN EXPERIENCES. EVERYONE'S LIFE IS A STOREHOUSE OF STORIES.

The power of parables is perhaps best illustrated in this story of the one university in the world that was built from the proceeds of one speech. The school is Temple University, and the speech, delivered by Russell Conwell, was called "Acres of Diamonds." His message was that diamonds, or nuggets of opportunity, are in your own backyard. Well, some fascinating things may happen to you if you dig up anecdotes and experiences in your background and use them in your speech.

One executive told me his bottom-line message to stockholders was more research. To reinforce that idea, he told in harrowing detail about how his brother had almost drowned in an ocean undertow. The family his brother was visiting at the shore had failed to research the area and thus didn't find out about the nasty currents that always appeared in the afternoon.

Look back on your own experiences. Everyone's life is a storehouse of stories.

Another CEO wanted to talk to his company's internal sales force about being at the right place at the right time. So I asked him how he met his wife.

Puzzled, he asked, "What does that have to do with anything, Humes?"

"Hey," I replied, "it's about being at the right place at the right time."

The material is right in front of them, yet a lot of CEOs are reluctant to tell stories about themselves. But when you share a bit of yourself with others, you win their trust and affection, and they will more readily buy into what you are promoting.

In my conversations with a CEO for whom I was writing a sales talk, I learned that he had been an All-Texas high school guard. In his remarks, he wanted to emphasize that persistence in sales calls would prevail over any promotional gimmicks by the main competitor.

> WHEN YOU SHARE A BIT OF YOURSELF WITH OTHERS, YOU WIN THEIR TRUST AND AFFECTION, AND THEY WILL MORE READILY BUY INTO WHAT YOU ARE PROMOTING.

So, I got him to talk about how on a rainy day his high school won, not by flashy long passes, but by ground plays three or four yards at a time.

If you have any point to put across, find a way to picture it in a story or parable.

A Case Story to Communicate Your Point

Try telling a real life story to flesh out your concept. If, for example, you want to make the point that your company must anticipate and be responsive to change, you might illustrate this concept by comparing two giant "five and ten cent" stores of the past century, Woolworth to Kresge.

Woolworth introduced the early retail stores and Kresge copied their success. But Woolworth didn't see soon enough that, in the emerging age of the shopping mall, the downtown store would die. Kresge did revamp itself—into K-Mart. Today Woolworth downtown stores are closing and K-Marts are opening in and near malls.

Let's say that you want to argue against recasting drastically. In other words, you want to say, "Don't change for the sake of change." Why not talk about Coca-Cola and their disastrous experiment in the 1970s, when they tampered with their "classic" formula in an attempt to appeal to younger tastes?

If your message is the repositioning of your company, you might mention the case of Marlborough, which in the 1940s packaged cigarettes for women but in the 1950s shortened the "Marlborough" to "Marlboro." Its advertising featured the Marlboro Man, a former football player who wore a ten-gallon hat and sat on a horse. The macho-man became the Marlboro Man.

Maybe you want to argue against repositioning. You might want to explain how Wedgwood China in the 1970s attempted to boost sales by going down-market with a cheaper version but instead ended up with expensive losses and eventually sold out to Waterford.

So pick out a business tale that will bolster your point. Check the back files of the *Wall Street Journal, New York Times* (Business Section), *Fortune,* or *Forbes* for parallels to your own company's situation. Then fit their story to your own marketing, sales, or research problem.

Parable power is persuasive power.

Power Gesture

*The greatest ruler acts as he speaks
and tailors his speech to his actions.*

—Confucius

In August 1964, Sir Winston Churchill lay dying in London's King Edward VII Hospital. General Eisenhower, who had just attended the twentieth anniversary of the D day invasion in France, visited his bedside. The venerable statesman, then in his ninetieth year, did not speak when Eisenhower entered his suite but instead reached out a frail pink hand to clasp Eisenhower's. The two hands joined on the bedside table.

No words were spoken—just two partners sharing silently the memories of their struggles in war and peace for the principles they both cherished. Ten minutes passed in silence. Two nations, two leaders, and two friends. Then Churchill unclasped his right hand and slowly moved it in a "vee for victory" sign!

Eisenhower, his eyes moist, left the room and told an aide:

I just said good-bye to Winston, but you never say farewell to courage.

Gestures Say More Than Words

Sometimes gestures say more than words. Other than Calvin Coolidge, the American president of fewest words was our first. George Washington was uncomfortable in speech. He grew up in the shadow of an older half-brother, Lawrence, whom he idolized. Lawrence had been educated at an English boarding school, and then commissioned in the Royal Navy. He possessed all the refinements of an English gentleman. George, back on the family farm with an almost illiterate mother, suffered by comparison.

George was six feet, three and a half inches tall by the time he was thirteen. He had the looks of a grown man, but his shyness and awkward speech belied his appearance. His solution was to talk as little as possible.

The Strong Silent Man

So Washington learned to make his actions speak for him. By doing so, he would become the prototype for the "strong silent man." At the turn of the last century, Owen Wister would write *The Virginian,* a novel about a Wyoming cowboy from Virginia. It engaged the imagination of early film writers. Years later movie stars Gary Cooper, John Wayne, and Clint Eastwood would all play heroes shaped by the Washington mold.

Washington demonstrated the power of his silence in 1781 when he was bidding his officers farewell at Fraunce's Tavern, near Wall Street in New York City, before he would board a boat that would take him back to Mount Vernon.

> WASHINGTON LEARNED TO MAKE HIS ACTIONS SPEAK FOR HIM. BY DOING SO, HE WOULD BECOME THE PROTOTYPE FOR THE "STRONG SILENT MAN."

At the tavern, Washington did not shake hands. Instead, he stopped by each officer, engaged the man's eyes, and then nodded. Then he passed on to the next. Some officers recorded in their diaries that it was the most meaningful moment in their life. A gesture may be a signal from the soul that words cannot convey.

The next time these officers saw Washington was in 1786, when he delivered another body signal that might well have averted a revolt. In a farmyard thirty miles west of Philadelphia, former Continental Army officers gathered to demand their back pay. They were threatening to mount an assault against the government in Philadelphia.

Washington rode up from Mount Vernon to confront them. He alit from his white stallion in the barnyard. Standing before the group of officers, the old general drew out a prepared statement from his cloak. Then he took some spectacles from his pocket and began:

> Gentlemen, I must apologize for my spectacles. My eyes have grown old in the service of my country.

The officers had never seen him wear glasses before. Some of them wept. After his short statement, the officers disbanded.

Twelve years later, in 1798, President Washington was striving to maintain neutrality in the war between Britain and France. Passions ran high in the new nation for coming to the aid of France, our former Revolutionary War ally. One evening a mob of three hundred, armed with clubs and guns, surged against the presidential mansion in Philadelphia. As they approached, Washington went to the front window and gazed out at the approaching rioters. His arms, folded across his chest, reinforced his cold stare.

When the ringleader came face-to-face with Washington, with only a windowpane between, he took one look at the resolute and contemptuous president and slinked away. The crowd of armed demonstrators followed him.

Again, a gesture succeeded when words might have failed.

A Master of Body Language

To liken the first United States president of this new century with our country's first-ever president would seem blasphemous to some—certainly in terms of character and integrity. Washington was a volunteer soldier whose public and private record reveals not one misrepresentation or lie.

Yet, like Washington, Bill Clinton is a master of body language. This is the secret of his communications magic. He has survived scandals that would have toppled others—Whitewater, the Monica Lewinsky mess, the close-to-a-million-dollar settlement with Paula Jones, the Juanita Broderick rape allegations, the rental of the Lincoln Bedroom, and, of course, the impeachment vote. And then the Arkansas disbarment proceedings on top of that.

Bill Clinton survived and prevailed because of his superb skills of projecting sincerity and commitment. He did this not with *what* he said but with *how* he said it.

Clinton has not coined any memorable lines such as Roosevelt or Kennedy did. Those presidents have dozens of sayings recorded in *Bartlett's Familiar Quotations.* Even the elder George Bush, whose forte was not eloquence, will be remembered for "a thousand points of light" and a "kinder and gentler nation" (phrases that came from the pen of Peggy Noonan).

Clinton, however, is the supreme artist in the creation and display of body signals. With body language, he bonded with the American people. His arsenal of physical cues include the biting of the lip to flash anguish, the looking up at the ceiling to suggest deep consideration of a question, the clenching of his jaw to manifest determination, and the pounding on the desk to signal angry

> BILL CLINTON SURVIVED AND PREVAILED BECAUSE OF HIS SUPERB SKILLS OF PROJECTING SINCERITY AND COMMITMENT. HE DID THIS NOT WITH *WHAT* HE SAID BUT WITH *HOW* HE SAID IT.

resolve. He could run the gamut from a broad grin to tears in seconds—as he did when the camera caught him smiling as he walked away from the memorial church service honoring his secretary of commerce Ron Brown, who had been killed in an air crash.

The Genius of Gesture

Whether TV viewers observed Clinton presenting an award to Eagle Scouts at a Rose Garden ceremony or making a classroom appearance with Afro-American students at a Washington school, they saw him radiating compassion and oozing commitment through body and facial language. He would hug the teacher and pat a kid's shoulders. He would nod approval to a comment or throw his head back in a chuckle to a jocular comment. Then he would open his mouth in wonderment at a tale of achievement.

But put him in the Oval Office for his weekly radio chat, and his speech fell flat. He needed people around him with whom to connect, on whom he could use a Power Gesture.

Personal Confession

Bill Clinton was best when he was having a conversation with his audience and body language was part of that conversation. Remember when he talked to an audience of black ministers? He talked to them as if he were on Oprah Winfrey's show. In "personal confession," he is supreme, and his gestures and expressions reinforce his penitence.

Clinton is unmatched in one-on-one sessions. A former Republican governor who became acquainted with Clinton when both were governors told me that he came away from a meeting sold, "as if I had found an alter-ego whose attitudes, ideas, and views were just like my own."

Bonding Through Body Language

In small group meetings, Clinton was just about as persuasive. Again, it was not his words but the physical ways in which he would establish communication with his listeners—the fixed-eye glance, the toss of a head, or a hand on the shoulder.

With such body language, Clinton projected a likeability and warmth, not only to the audience in the Rose Garden or Oval Office, but also to the TV audience watching clips of such sessions on the evening news. Body language was the power that propelled Clinton's approval ratings upward.

Clinton's most famous gesture was wielded to enforce his most noted and quoted statement. At that press conference in January 1998, he pointed his index finger as he said, "I have never had sex with that woman."

The wagging finger enforced the credibility of a statement that was a lie. It only proves how powerful one body signal can be.

But it is not necessary for an executive to try to develop his or her leadership potential by practicing all kinds of hand or face movements. In fact, if you are not a professional actor, trying them would be self-defeating. Concentrate on just one gesture for a meeting or talk.

The Right Signal at the Right Time

One gesture may be all it takes to get your point across. Some years ago the chairman and chief executive of a bakery company had just completed successful negotiations in buying another bakery in an adjoining state, a deal that would ensure bigger profits and growth for the future. The board members, who were aware of the proposed merger, looked at him when

> ONE GESTURE MAY BE ALL IT TAKES TO GET YOUR POINT ACROSS.

he walked into the conference room, but his face showed no expression. As he got to his chair, he gave a thumbs-up sign and his mouth stretched into a big grin.

The CEO's later explanation of financial details was almost anticlimactic. The thumbs-up epitomized his leadership style. The right signal can magnify a speaking moment.

The quintessential memory of the great comedian Jack Benny is his deadpan turning aside when the robber asks him, "Your money or your life?"

Then, after some seconds, Benny says, "I'm thinking, I'm thinking."

Remember how Johnny Carson directed his eyes to the ceiling with that perplexed grin of his? This was his classic reaction to the diminutive and aged sexologist Dr. Ruth Westheimer when she explained the nature of an orgasm.

Sometimes the right gesture speaks more eloquently than words. Senator John McCain returned in April 2000 to the "Vietnam Hilton," where he was once held prisoner. It is now a museum that parades pictures of happy and smiling prisoners. McCain pointed out one photograph of a grinning prisoner scratching his chin with only the middle finger of his hand. The prisoner's face may have been smiling at his Vietcong captors, but his gesture conveyed to Americans an altogether different attitude.

> SOMETIMES THE RIGHT GESTURE SPEAKS MORE ELOQUENTLY THAN WORDS.

Ronald Reagan defeated President Carter with the perfect gesture in his 1980 debate. After Carter attacked him, Reagan delivered his patented cock of the head with a smile and uttered, "There you go again."

When the Pencil Is Mightier Than the Sword

President Eisenhower had a way of expressing displeasure without saying a word. For example, Secretary of Agriculture Benson was once fulminating on a matter of foreign policy in a cabinet meeting. Because this was outside the secretary's realm of expertise, the president began stabbing the tablet with his pencil and then he looked at the ceiling with a grimace. Benson stopped.

In the Eisenhower era, an act that got a lot of attention was one by Eisenhower's Russian counterpart in the Cold War, Nikita Khruschev. At the United Nations, when a litany of Soviet Union human rights violations was being detailed by Ambassador Henry Cabot Lodge, the Soviet chairman took off his shoe and banged it on the table before him. British prime minister Harold Mac-Millan then dryly asked, "May we have a translation?"

And then there's the most notorious gesture in history: Pontius Pilate washing his hands after the Sanhedrin's guilty verdict on Christ.

Acts by the body can count more than words. Silent signals can register even louder than speech.

> **SILENT SIGNALS CAN REGISTER EVEN LOUDER THAN SPEECH.**

Executives as well as politicians can benefit by putting this knowledge to good use. For example, a pipe-smoking executive with a leading mineral company built his career as a union negotiator through body language. He would fold his hands tentlike to show interest in a proposal. Then he would stroke his chin to signal his consideration of it. If he was skeptical, he would cross his arms in front of his shoulders. The ultimate rejection was his pounding ashes out of his pipe. Though he was the ranking executive of the corporate team, he would let others do most of the talking. But his cues were signals for them to start translating his gestures into words.

Another executive I knew once opened a company meeting by pointing his finger like a pistol, aiming, and firing three times. He followed up by outlining three ways they were going to "kill" their chief competitor: "by lower costs" (he cocked his finger in trigger action), "by better marketing" (he cocked it again), "and by a new advertising campaign" (and he flashed his index finger as a pistol once again).

Finding the Right Exhibit

Sometimes it is not so much exhibiting the right pose as finding the right exhibit. A woman executive wanted to dramatize the cost of government regulation to a business. At a trade association breakfast meeting, she carried to the front of the table piles of huge sheets of paper tied with rubber bands. Then she dropped them on the table in front of her with a thud. After a pause, she announced:

> These are copies of all the regulations from the Federal Register. Some of them conflict with each other, but we have to comply with all of them. These are taxes, not only of our money, but of our time and personnel.

Ben's Briefcase of Bills

Benjamin Franklin, America's first self-made millionaire, was no orator. In fact, he often preferred symbols to words. He once advised a merchant to tear down this sign: "John Thompson Hatter Makes and Sells Hats for Ready Cash and Money." Franklin then told the merchant: "Thompson, put up a new one with just a picture of a hat."

Franklin was without peer as a negotiator, as this story demonstrates:

> At the end of the Revolutionary War, he headed the diplomatic team that went to Paris to work out a treaty with the British.
>
> The Americans wanted all the British territory to the Mississippi, fishing rights off New England and Canada, and non-harassment of our commercial ships on the high seas.
>
> These were uphill negotiations because the British had the power to leave the situation in limbo. They had little to gain by formally recognizing the new American government. Yet Franklin succeeded in hammering out an agreement with the British. But when the time came for putting pen to treaty, Lord Shelburne balked and began to walk out of the Round Room at Lansdowne House in London.

"Just a minute," said Franklin. "First you better settle your bill." And Franklin dug into his traveling case and pulled out, one by one, hundreds of itemized records—of houses requisitioned, warehouses taken over, barns burned, wagons appropriated, and horses seized.

Shelburne looked at them, sighed, and then signed, saying, "You're a hard man, Franklin."

With one dramatic gesture, Franklin forced the British to sign the treaty recognizing the new thirteen freed colonies as a nation.

Leadership sometimes demands more than verbiage. It requires visible acts. Chose and use a Power Gesture.

> LEADERSHIP SOMETIMES DEMANDS MORE THAN VERBIAGE. IT REQUIRES VISIBLE ACTS.

Power Reading

First he read his speech,
second he read it badly,
third it wasn't worth reading.
—WINSTON CHURCHILL

Ronald Reagan was the Great Communicator, right? Actually, he was fired from his first communications job!

After Reagan got his degree at Eureka College in Illinois, he answered an ad for a radio station in Iowa. Surely his resonant baritone and acting experience in college helped convince his new employer. Over the airwaves, Reagan did project a warm personality with an easy flow of cheery conversation.

So why did the station fire him? Because he was a flop at reading the commercials. The automobile and department store advertisers didn't like the way he read their ads. The vivacity left his voice. He was wooden and flat.

It was the Great Depression, and Reagan was out of work. In his rented room he thought long and hard. He liked his radio job and wanted it back. The solution came from his hero, President Roosevelt, whose Fireside Chats Reagan regularly tuned in to on his radio. Roosevelt, he knew, was reading from a text. Yet he sounded so conversational and so believable!

Reagan tried reading the president's speeches for practice. He discovered that if he looked down at a phrase or short sentence and then repeated it without looking down, he could simulate Roosevelt's easy, flowing style. The pause between each scanning of the phrase in the newspaper page before uttering it aloud didn't make him sound stilted. In fact, it was more in keeping with Roosevelt's own rhythm.

The technique wasn't new to Reagan. At college he had done it while auditioning for roles in plays. He had landed the best roles because he looked at the play director while reading his lines, while the other students did not.

Memorize Then Conversationalize

He then practiced reading the newspaper ads the same way. He would look down at a line or two, then look away at the wall in his room and "conversationalize" the line he had just read.

When the commentator who had taken over Reagan's job took a job at another station, Reagan asked for a second chance. This time, when doing the commercials, he would look down to memorize a line or two ("Bill's Pontiac is offering a great deal") and then he would cover the ad with his hands, look up, and conversationalize the memorized line into the microphone.

Reagan would then look down again and memorize the next line ("Why, for only $200 you can drive away a brand new Pontiac coupe"), and then conversationalize that line for the microphone.

The new technique made him a hit with the radio advertisers. Reagan had discovered the secret of the two greatest masters of communication in the century: Franklin Roosevelt and Winston Churchill.

Not uncoincidentally, both were shaped by the same man. Bourke Cockrane is not a familiar name even to students of American history, yet this Irish immigrant to

New York City, who became the country's greatest trial lawyer, was a mentor to these two great leaders of the twentieth century.

Anthologies of eloquence carry Cockrane's orations. Thrice he was the keynoter for the Democratic National Convention. Yet he broke with his party to endorse Theodore Roosevelt in 1904. Churchill, who met him first in New York in 1905, called him "the single greatest influence in my life."

A dying Cockrane would ask his protégé Franklin Roosevelt to deliver in his place the nominating speech for Governor Al Smith at the Democratic National Convention in 1924. "Get off your sick bed, Frank, and give the speech."

The eloquent introduction of Smith ("I give to you the Happy Warrior . . .") would catapult the polio-stricken Roosevelt back into the national limelight.

> **BOURKE COCKRANE PERFECTED THE ART OF READING A SPEECH WHILE APPEARING NOT TO, A SECRET HE WOULD SHARE WITH CHURCHILL AND ROOSEVELT.**

Congressman Bourke Cockrane, who was a distant kin of the great parliamentary orator Edmund Burke, had perfected the art of reading a speech while appearing not to. He would share this secret with Churchill and Roosevelt.

Don't Speak While Looking Down

The first rule of effective speaking, Cockrane told both Churchill and Roosevelt, is this:

Never, never, never let words come out of your mouth when your eyes are looking down.

Have you ever stepped on a wire and stopped the current? Well, when you are looking down and speaking, you are disconnecting the current of your words to your listeners. You must be *looking* at your listeners when you are talking to them.

A business executive who knows how to read from a text is exceedingly rare. That is no surprise. But I am surprised at how few politicians have taken the time to master the art—especially since most politicians have two speeches: their standard one, which they know by heart, and the one prepared for them, which they read.

My friend, former vice presidential candidate Jack Kemp, dazzles audiences with his tried-and-true "free market" address but can be dull when he reads from a text on another subject. In contrast, Ted Kennedy, Henry Kissinger, and William F. Buckley Jr. come to mind as political celebrities who have mastered the art of reading speeches from a text.

Business executives often tell me they *have to* read their speeches. The chief executives of the biggest banks, insurance companies, pharmaceutical companies, oil companies, airlines, and airplane manufacturers are almost compelled to read their speeches, they argue, by the scope of their corporate liability. House counsels have nightmares about their CEOs delivering some unscripted remark that journalists might seize upon to show their insensitivity and greed. Or worse, the CEO might have an unfortunate lapse that would support a billion-dollar class-action suit. One miscue in an off-the-cuff comment could bring down the angry arm of Uncle Sam in the form of an anti-trust regulatory action.

> **WHEN YOU ARE LOOKING DOWN WHILE SPEAKING, YOU ARE DISCONNECTING THE CURRENT OF YOUR WORDS TO YOUR LISTENERS. YOU MUST BE LOOKING AT YOUR LISTENERS WHEN YOU ARE TALKING TO THEM.**

To avoid such lapses or miscues, companies often have a team of speechwriters write a set of prepared remarks, which is then sent to the general counsel's office and is next run by the vice president for public affairs. When friends and acquaintances of the business leaders hear him read the finished product, they are puzzled that this executive, whom they find so strong and forceful in private conversation, is so wooden in his public presentation.

When counseling a CEO, I make it a rule to videotape him when he is talking informally about his company and the principal problems facing his industry. Then I videotape him reading a speech of current business interest. The comparison is always dramatic—when the CEO is conversational, he's dynamic; when he reads a talk, he drones.

> **WHEN THE CEO IS CONVERSATIONAL, HE'S DYNAMIC; WHEN HE READS A TALK, HE DRONES.**

Even when the executive tries to put force into his delivery, it sounds more artificial than authoritative. He is speaking *at* us, not *to* us. He is not looking at us in the audience. The pace of delivery is both too rapid and too unvaried to seem like the natural flow of conversation.

Al Gore had this problem as vice president. Gore seemed to have only two buttons on his voice box: drone and shout!

See—Stop—Say Technique

The solution to ineffective reading is to adopt the Churchill/Roosevelt/Reagan method, which I call the See—Stop—Say technique.

For practice, take out your *Wall Street Journal.* Pick out an editorial or op-ed column. Then set up a makeshift lectern such as a box or a drawer on top of a table and place the article on the box or bottom of the drawer as you would a speech to be read.

Look down and take an imaginary "snapshot" of the words you *see.* Bring your head back up and *pause.* Then, while looking at a lamp or other object at the far end of the room as if it was a listener, *say,* or "conversationalize," what you have just memorized. Then look down again to see the next chunk of words, bring your head back up and pause, and then speak. See, Stop, Say.

If you have tried the See—Stop—Say plan, you'll be saying, as one executive told me, "Humes, these pauses while I bring my head up to speak, and then when I look down to memorize the next few lines, make me feel awkward. It makes my speaking sort of jerky, and that pause is going to make me lose my audience. Their minds are going to turn to something else."

Wrong! Sure, the pause does let you read the speech in segments while still fixing your eyes on the audience. But the real power of the pause is that it gives your listeners time to digest what you're saying.

If you've ever run out of gas and poured gas from a can back into the tank, you'll recall how the narrow tube often rejects it and triggers a backflow or overflow. In the same way, a listener rejects a speech that's read. Not only does it sound boring, but without a pause, an overfilled ear turns off.

Listen to any conversation. You don't speak nonstop. You take pauses. Those pauses are what make a speech sound conversational. Listen to tapes of Churchill, Roosevelt, and Reagan. Their delivery is not nonstop. Check out tapes of orators like Congresswoman Barbara Jordan or General Douglas MacArthur. Note their pauses. The effect is deliberative, statesmanlike. In fact, the pause is your most powerful tool in speaking.

So let's try the exercise of reading that article again.

> **PAUSES ARE WHAT MAKE A SPEECH SOUND CONVERSATIONAL.**

Look down and *see* the words. Bring your head up and *stop* for a second. Then *say* the line in your own words.

Why must you pause after you bring your head up? Because most speakers start to speak while their heads are moving up. They think the pause has been too long so are anxious to begin speaking again. But by taking that extra second pause, you fool the audience into thinking that you are just glancing at notes and not actually reading the speech.

The pause may seem like an eternity to you, but to your audience it is a microsecond—a microsecond that "punctuates" the sentence, builds audience anticipation, and helps listener understanding.

Does the pause still sound labored and stilted? Does it still seem artificially jarring to you? Maybe it does to you, but to your audience you'll be sounding like Winston Churchill, Franklin Roosevelt, or Ronald Reagan.

Not Awkward but Authentic

If you still don't believe me, have someone videotape you, and then watch yourself. The corporate executives I coach are always amazed when they see themselves on the screen. The pause they thought felt so awkward makes their delivery sound more like their conversational style.

> WHEN YOU PAUSE, YOU SOUND SINCERE, AS IF YOU'RE TRYING TO COME UP WITH THE RIGHT WORDS TO EXPRESS YOUR THOUGHTS.

In our conversations, we often pause to think of the right words, to organize our thoughts, to frame the next sentence.

When you read a speech without pauses, you seem to be reading a speech someone else wrote for you. When you pause, you sound sincere, as if you're trying to come up with the right words to express your thoughts.

Try the See—Stop—Say technique again. Look down. *See* the text. Look up—all the way up—and *Stop.* Then *Say* that phrase you've just recorded in your mind. Continue this technique for the rest of the editorial or article.

At first you may remember to bring you head back up and pause, but after some minutes of speaking you'll find yourself sliding back into starting to speak before your head is *all* the way back up.

Don't worry. Keep practicing.

Physical, Not Mental

When I teach corporate executives this See—Stop—Say technique, who do you think picks up the method the quickest? MENSA qualifiers? Rocket scientists? Lawyers or engineers? What about women as opposed to men? Intellectual introverts or backslapping extroverts?

The answer is "jocks"—in other words, men or women who are good at golf, tennis, or some other sport. Basically, the technique is not a mental, but an eye-hand skill. Television anchorpersons are not necessarily picked for their brains, but they're pros at reading texts.

That does not mean that you have to be a natural athlete to read a speech. Actually, the See—Stop—Say plan for reading a speech is easier than riding a bike. If you've ever played golf or tennis, you're likely to recall how strange a new grip the club pro taught you seemed at first, but then, with practice, it eventually felt normal. Similarly, with practice you'll soon find it easy to See—Stop—Say while reading your speech.

> WITH PRACTICE YOU'LL SOON FIND IT EASY TO SEE—STOP—SAY WHILE READING YOUR SPEECH.

Let's do the exercise again:

Look down and take in a line.
Look up and pause.
Deliver the line.
Look down and take in another line.
Look up and pause.
Deliver another line.

Remember that the pause is the major tool in reading a speech. It not only helps you "eye-photograph" your text, phrase by phrase, but also lets the audience digest your words better.

To try out the technique, read this excerpt from Churchill's "Iron Curtain" speech given in 1946:

A shadow had fallen upon the scene

[pause]

so lately lighted by the Allied victory

[pause]

From Stettin in the Baltic
to Trieste in the Adriatic

[pause]

an iron curtain had descended across the continent.

So read a speech like Reagan—and sell your audience. Recite a talk like Roosevelt—and persuade your listeners.

13

Power Poetry

Who says in verse what others say in prose?
—ALEXANDER POPE

Winston Churchill was once handed a speech that he had dictated. He glanced at it and growled, "Who's been ending my lines with 'of's' and 'the's'"? It was Churchill's obsession that a speech should not sound like an article read aloud, and neither should it be typed up the way an article is.

An article looks like most of this page. The line has to end when space runs out. Churchill would argue that an article should be written for the eye, but a speech for the ear.

"Speech Is Verse"

Churchill once said:

Every speech is a rhymeless, meterless verse.

And when giving a speech from text, Churchill wanted to be able to read it as if it were laid out like poetry.

Churchill delivered his "Fall of France" speech to the House of Commons of June 4, 1940. The distinguished author A. P. Herbert, who was also a member of Parliament, described Churchill's speech:

> I have been moved in theaters and churches but never so deeply. Those famous phrases passed into history as he offered them.

Here is an excerpt of the speech as it appears in an anthology of Churchill's notable addresses.

> What General Weygand called the Battle of France is over. I expect that the Battle of Britain is about to begin. Upon this battle depends the survival of Christian civilization. Upon it depends our own British life, and the long continuity of our institutions and our Empire. The whole fury and might of the enemy must very soon be turned on us. Hitler knows that he will have to break us in this Island or lose the war. If we can stand up to him, all Europe may be free and the life of the whole world may move forward into broad, sunlit uplands. But if we fail, then the whole world, including the United States, including all that we have known and cared for, will sink into the abyss of a new Dark Age, made more sinister, and perhaps more protracted, by the lights of perverted science. Let us therefore brace ourselves to our duties, and so bear ourselves that, if the British Empire and its Commonwealth last for a thousand years, men will say, "This was their finest hour."

CHURCHILL WOULD ARGUE THAT AN ARTICLE SHOULD BE WRITTEN FOR THE EYE, BUT A SPEECH FOR THE EAR.

Now look at the actual text Churchill read from when he spoke in the House of Commons.

> What General Weygand called
> the Battle of France is over.
> I expect that the Battle of Britain
> is about to begin.
> Upon this battle
> depends the survival of Christian civilization.
> Upon it depends our own British life

and the long continuity of our institutions
and our Empire.
The whole fury and might of the enemy
must very soon be turned on us.
Hitler knows
that he will have to break us in this Island
or lose the war.
If we can stand up to him,
all Europe may be free
and the life of the whole world
may move forward into broad, sunlit uplands.
But if we fail,
then the whole world,
including the United States,
including all that we have known and cared for,
will sink into the abyss of a new Dark Age
made more sinister, and perhaps more protracted,
by the lights of perverted science.
Let us therefore brace ourselves to our duties
and so bear ourselves
that, if the British Empire and its Commonwealth
last for a thousand years,
men will say
"This was their finest hour."

Transform a Speech into Poetry

Churchill knew the secret of Power Poetry.

> IF SPEECH IS PROSE, THE PHRASE-BY-PHRASE TECHNIQUE CAN TRANSFORM IT INTO POETRY.

If speech is prose, the phrase-by-phrase technique can transform it into poetry.

Let's look at the speech that the poet Carl Sandburg called "the great American poem": the Gettysburg Address, which is the most memorized and most recited speech in all history.

On November 19, 1993, the 130th anniversary of the address, I was asked to deliver it on the steps of the Lincoln Memorial in Washington. Winston Churchill II, in his introduction of me, said his grandfather had termed the address "the ultimate expression of the majesty of Shakespeare's language."

My recitation was followed by a resonant rendition of "The Battle Hymn of the Republic" by Ambassador Alan Keyes. Later Keyes, an orator of no mean distinction, told me that he had never heard the address better delivered.

The secret was how I had the text laid out before me.

Fourscore and seven years ago
our fathers brought forth upon this continent
a new nation
conceived in liberty
and dedicated to the proposition
that all men are created equal.
Now we are engaged in a great civil war,
testing whether that nation or any nation
so conceived and so dedicated
can long endure.
We are met on a great battlefield of that war.
We have come to dedicate a portion of that field
as a final resting place
for those who gave their lives
that this nation might live.
It is altogether fitting and proper that we should do this.
But in a larger sense,
we cannot dedicate—
we cannot consecrate—
we cannot hallow this ground.
The brave men, living and dead,
who struggled here
have consecrated it
far beyond our poor power

to add or detract.
The world will little note
nor long remember
what we say here,
but it can never forget
what they did here.
It is for us the living
rather to be dedicated here
to the unfinished work
which they who fought here
have thus far so nobly advanced.
It is rather for us to be here dedicated
to the great task remaining before us
that from these honored dead
we take increased devotion
to that cause for which
they gave the last full measure of devotion—
that we here highly resolve:
that these dead shall not have died in vain,
that this nation under God
shall have a new birth of freedom—
and that government
of the people
by the people
and for the people
shall not perish from the earth.

Make Your Layout Luminous

When you look at this layout of phrases, mark how the parallel wording leaps out at you.

> <u>conceived</u> in liberty and
> <u>dedicated</u> to the proposition . . .

Note the poetic consonance of the letter "V"

for those who <u>gave</u> their <u>lives</u> that this nation might <u>live</u>

Listen to the internal rhyme in these parallel phrases.

we cannot <u>dedicate</u>
we cannot <u>consecrate</u>

Look how the alliterative words catch your attention.

will <u>little</u> note
nor <u>long</u> remember

See how the spacing of the parallel prepositional phrases helps the reciter of the address.

of the people
by the people
and for the people

Tenets for Typing

For any talk, little or long—an introduction or a chamber of commerce talk, a press announcement, an in-house pep talk—take your typed speech and space it out in bite-size phrases.

My students at the Universities of Pennsylvania and Southern Colorado were given these rules for typing out their text.

> **"FOR ANY TALK, LITTLE OR LONG, TAKE YOUR TYPED SPEECH AND SPACE IT OUT IN BITE-SIZE PHRASES."**

- When you come to a comma, cut the line off!

- If your subject is followed by its predicate, don't separate them.

- When a preposition is succeeded by its object, don't dissect the two!

- Never end a line with "a" or "the."

- When you see a period, make sure to call a halt.

Another Churchill anecdote illustrates the importance of speech-appropriate punctuation:

Churchill in a cabinet meeting once looked over at a speech that his foreign secretary Anthony Eden had before him on the table.

"It's a bad speech, Anthony," Churchill remarked.

"How can you tell?" replied Eden. "Surely you can't read up-side down, Prime Minister!"

"I can tell," replied Churchill, "because there are too many semicolons and never a dash."

Churchill believed that in remarks directed to the ear, a semicolon was verboten—whereas a dash fit the rhythm of a speech or talk, making it more conversational.

Let's examine part of the opening of Kennedy's inaugural address in 1961 and see how Churchill might have adapted it to Power Poetry spacing.

> CHURCHILL BELIEVED THAT IN REMARKS DIRECTED TO THE EAR, A SEMICOLON WAS VERBOTEN—WHEREAS A DASH FIT THE RHYTHM OF A SPEECH OR TALK.

We observe today not a victory of party but a celebration of freedom—symbolizing an end as well as a beginning, signifying renewal as well as change. For I have sworn before you and Almighty God the same solemn oath our forebears prescribed nearly a century and three-quarters ago. The world is very different now. For man holds in his mortal hands the power to abolish all forms of human poverty and all forms of human life. And yet the same revolutionary beliefs for which our forebears fought are still at issue around the globe.

Now putting this text into Power Poetry, and spacing it in the right way on the typed page, is not rocket science but common sense. Let's see how the spacing looks on the page.

We observe today
not a victory of party
but a celebration of freedom—
symbolizing an end
as well as a beginning,
signifying renewal as well as change.
For I have sworn before you and Almighty God
the same solemn oath
our forebears prescribed

nearly a century and three-quarters ago.
The world is very different now.
For man holds in his mortal hands
the power to abolish all forms of human poverty
and all forms of human life.
And yet the same revolutionary belief
for which our forbears fought
are still at issue around the globe.

Churchill once said a speech is "poetry without form or rhyme." The Kennedy inaugural is proof of this.

But look how the following lay out of another portion of Kennedy's address brings out the intrinsic poetry—rhythm, rhyme, and alliteration—as though with a highlighter.

Let every nation know,
whether it wishes us <u>well</u> or <u>ill</u>
that we shall <u>pay</u> any <u>price</u>,
<u>bear</u> any <u>burden</u>,
support any <u>friend</u>,
oppose any <u>foe</u>,
to assure the <u>survival</u>
and the <u>success</u> of liberty.

Of course, none of you is likely to deliver an inaugural address, but you are going to make introductions, present awards, or explain business proposals. You will have the opportunity to enhance your speaking with elements of poetry, as I did in this introduction I wrote for Elizabeth Dole.

"Elizabeth." It's a regal name!
Think of Queen Elizabeth the First—
the greatest monarch of the Renaissance.
Like her namesake,
Elizabeth Dole has administered dynamically
in the realms of government,

the Departments of Labor and Transportation.
But Elizabeth is a poetic
as well as a regal name.
Think of the greatest English poetess,
Elizabeth Barrett Browning,
who wrote those enduring words:
"How do I love thee?
Let me count the ways."
Well, Elizabeth Dole manifests
the poignancy of a poet,
the soul of a Samaritan,
and the heart of a humanitarian
in the way she answers the needs
of those who are flood-damaged,
hurricane-ravaged,
and plague-afflicted.
Finally, think of Elizabeth Cady Stanton,
the first and greatest pioneer
for women's rights.
Well, in her career, Elizabeth Dole—
as a lawyer,
as White House advisor,
as cabinet member,
as American Red Cross president—
is an object of admiration,
a role for emulation,
a source of inspiration
for all women—
and for that matter men too.
I give you a great American
who leads
with her head,
her hands,
and her heart—
Elizabeth Dole.

See how the spacing makes it easier for you to read and easier for your listener to absorb the words.

Take a look at the following awards ceremony talk I drafted for a presenter of a plaque to Oriole star Cal Ripken, Jr. Notice how the spacing enables the speaker to phrase his talk like poetry.

Baseball is the sport of statistics
And the record of all records
Belongs to Cal—
The Most Consecutive Games Played!
It is a feat
Of epic achievement,
Of heroic proportions,
Of miraculous dimensions.
Yet there might be a secret to his stamina—
A source for the strength—
Of this man who was born in Aberdeen,
A little town on the Chesapeake Bay.
All of us in Maryland know that
The Susquehanna River empties into that bay.
But do you know where that river begins?
It begins in upstate New York
As a trickle of a little stream—
A couple of miles from Cooperstown.
You see, Cal Ripken all his life
Has been nourished by the waters
From the Hall of Fame.
I give you Hall of Famer
Born and bred, Cal Ripken.

Let the Layout Leap Out at You

Again, the layout lets the key words and phrases leap out at you. You don't have to be glued to the text.

To see another illustration of the power of proper layout, take note of these brief remarks I drafted for a bank president for a fifty-year anniversary celebration of the bank's founding:

As Abraham Lincoln would say,
"Twoscore and ten years ago
Mahlon Thatcher brought forth upon this city
A new bank."
I mention Lincoln
for he was fabled in his grocery store
for once walking six miles to return four cents.
Well, our founder, Mahlon Thatcher,
was also known for his friendliness and his service.
One day a customer, a farmer, had a flat tire
right next to the bank.
He looked in his trunk.
He had no tire iron.
Then an old guy with balding gray hair
   and dressed in a lumberjack shirt
noticed his predicament and said,
"I have one in my car. You take it."
"Don't you need it?"
said the distressed farmer.
"Oh yes, just return it to the bank tomorrow."
The man did just that.
The next day he asked the teller,
"Where's the janitor?"
"We have no janitor," was the puzzled reply.
"Can you describe the person?" asked the clerk.
"Well, he's an oldish sort of guy,
getting a little bald,
gray around the edges."
"Oh, you mean Mr. Thatcher.
He's the president."
And for fifty years
the feature of this bank has been friendliness
and its signature service.

> **THE LAYOUT LETS THE KEY WORDS AND PHRASES LEAP OUT AT YOU. YOU DON'T HAVE TO BE GLUED TO THE TEXT.**

Mahlon Thatcher died years ago,
But that tradition lives on today
In this bank.

Churchill, as I discuss in my book *Churchill: Speaker of the Century,* discovered this secret of changing the old typed article layout into a format approaching that of verse.

Students tell me that this way of laying out a talk into phrases is the most useful advice they have taken away from my Language of Leadership class. One student told me:

> Professor Humes, it made me focus on the fact that it was an oral presentation that I was to deliver—that I couldn't just write an article and read it aloud.

Change your format to Churchill's. Lay out your lines like a leader, and you'll sound like one.

14

Power Line

These words like daggers enter in my ears.
—WILLIAM SHAKESPEARE

In *Bartlett's Familiar Quotations,* more pages of quotations belong to Winston Churchill than any other author of the twentieth century.

John Kennedy once said: "Churchill mobilized the English language and sent it into his battle." His words steeled his countrymen's resolve. The historian, Arnold Toynbee wrote this of Churchill: "His speeches spelled the difference between survival and defeat." His wartime addresses contained many memorable lines, what I call Power Lines.

There is a secret to coining a Power Line. And I doubt it will surprise you that Winston Churchill reportedly came up with a formula that's easily remembered by its acronym: C-R-E-A-M, which stands for Contrast—Rhyme—Echo—Alliteration—Metaphor. Just as cream rises to the top in a bottle of unhomogenized milk, the lines created with these five elements will stay uppermost in a listener's mind.

Opposites Attract

For *Contrast,* note this Churchill quotation:

> If the present quarrels with the past, surely the future will already have been lost.

Another Churchill use of contrast is his statement after the British victory in Egypt at Tobruk in 1942.

> This is not the end, nay, not even the beginning of the end, but it is, perhaps, the end of the beginning.

Churchill also minted this memorable line:

> There is only one answer to defeat and that is victory.

If you want to coin your own Power Line, try pairing these antonyms. Take one word for the first part of the sentence and then its opposite for the second part.

Present	—	Past (or Future)
Beginning	—	End
Dark	—	Light
Mountain	—	Valley
Rich	—	Poor
Friend	—	Foe
Gain	—	Loss
Hope	—	Despair
Victory	—	Defeat
Day	—	Night
Win	—	Lose
Sunshine	—	Shadow
Truth	—	Lies
Plant	—	Reap
Triumph	—	Tragedy
Save	—	Spend
Laugh	—	Cry
War	—	Peace

The late Hubert Humphrey, one of the Democratic Party's finest orators in the last century, used this technique. At the party convention in Philadelphia in 1948, his civil rights speech caused a walkout of the Southern Democrats. His ringing oration carried this Power Line:

> Let us move out of the <u>shadow</u> of states' rights into the <u>sunshine</u> of human rights.

Abraham Lincoln wielded contrasting words in this Power Line. He explained his political stance when he opposed the extension of slavery:

> As I would not be a <u>slave</u>, so I would not be a <u>master</u>.

> **THERE IS A SECRET TO COINING A POWER LINE: C-R-E-A-M, WHICH STANDS FOR CONTRAST— RHYME—ECHO— ALLITERATION— METAPHOR.**

Alexander Hamilton in his draft for Washington's Farewell Address in 1797 paired these antonyms for this aphorism:

> The best means of insuring <u>peace</u> is to be prepared for <u>war</u>.

By the time of the American Revolution, Benjamin Franklin had spawned a large collection of quotations— punchy maxims that he used to liven up the pages on weather and crops in his *Almanac*. He called them "The Sayings of Poor Richard." (Richard Saunders was the fictional editor of Franklin's *Almanac*. Franklin posed only as the printer, for he didn't want to get blamed for inaccurate weather forecasts!) Contrast was a favorite technique of Franklin's. Here are several examples of "Poor Richard" adages using contrast:

> Half the <u>truth</u> is often a great <u>lie</u>.

> There never was a <u>good</u> <u>war</u> or <u>bad</u> <u>peace</u>.

> If you would keep your secret from an <u>enemy</u>, tell it not to a <u>friend</u>.

> Never leave that for <u>tomorrow</u> which you can do <u>today</u>.

It is easy to craft an outstanding line with opposites. For example, I supplied this line for a CEO to include in an annual report for a stockholders' meeting:

> If the fantastic growth statistics for the past year, 1987, are any guide, we have unbounded hopes for the future."

Rhyme Is the Prime Ploy

The second phrase technique Churchill sometimes exploited—*Rhyme*—is perhaps the most ancient of storyteller's tricks. Homer, the Hellenic blind poet, ensured that bards in future generations would tell his tales of *The Iliad* and *The Odyssey* by chanting rhymes with lyre accompaniment.

In what some would call Churchill's greatest speech, at Fulton, Missouri, on March 5, 1946, note how he sets up the phrase "Iron Curtain" with a rhyme of two seas.

> From Stettin in the Baltic to Trieste in the Adriatic, an iron curtain has descended upon the continent of Europe.

That illustrates the use of the internal rhyme—more subtle than the hard-beat rhymes of the nursery. Here's another use of internal rhyme by Churchill:

> Out of intense complexities, intense simplicities emerge.
> Humanity, not legality, should be our guide.

Churchill also would mock his socialist foes with these rhyming nouns:

> These professional intellectuals who revel in decimals and polysyllables . . .

Benjamin Franklin, with his Poor Richard sayings, preferred more obvious sing-song rhymes, such as these:

> An apple a day keeps the doctor away.

> Little strokes fell great oaks.

Or perhaps his most quoted maxim:

Early to bed, early to rise, makes a man healthy, wealthy, and wise.

Franklin Roosevelt, in vetoing an act of Congress, also used rhyme when he declared:

This is not an act providing relief for the needy but for the greedy.

In modern times, Jesse Jackson has built a career as a civil rights activist by rousing audiences with rhymes such as this one:

There is no hope for those who use dope.

Ted Sorensen, a speechwriter for Kennedy, told me he kept on his desk, as Churchill did, a rhyming dictionary (a pocket edition that you can purchase for five dollars). For Kennedy to use in his inaugural address, Sorensen penned this feminine rhyme (a rhyme in which the strong syllable is the next to the last one):

Let both sides explore what problems unite us instead of belaboring those problems that divide us.

On another occasion Sorensen drafted this sentence for Kennedy:

In a world of mass extermination, nations must turn to the rule of self-determination.

Former president Richard Nixon wrote this subtle rhyme in 1984:

Faith may move mountains, but faith without might is futile and might without faith is sterile.

Dr. Martin Luther King, well known for his poetic speeches, wrote this from the Birmingham jail:

Injustice anywhere is a threat to justice everywhere.

Rhyming Nine

Versifiers as well as speechwriters often turn to the Rhyming Nine—AME, AIR, ITE, AKE, OW, AY, ATE, EEM, AIN—for coining "zinger" lines.

Here are the nine, along with some examples:

1. **AME**: aim, blame, claim, fame, name, shame, same, game, reclaim proclaim, flame

   I heard one executive say this to his board:

   We cannot remain the <u>same</u> company unless we <u>reclaim</u> the market we once had.

2. **AIR**: bear, care, dare, fare, fair, share, aware, swear, pare, declare, where, scare, prayer, beware

3. **ITE**: bite, cite, fight, fright, height, light, night, right, quite, sight, write, delight foresight, ignite, tonight

   At an annual meeting I attended, a CEO announced:

   If we are going to make it work—to do it <u>right</u>—the only real and right course is to keep our goals in <u>sight</u>.

4. **AKE**: ache, break, fake, sake, shake, stake, take, make, awake, undertake, mistake

   I heard an executive say this:

   Make no <u>mistake</u>, much is at <u>stake</u> in this new venture.

5. **OW**: dough, flow, foe, glow, go, grow, know, low, show, slow, throw, ago

6. **AY**: day, pray, stay, say, way, pay, play, away, stray, they, array, display

7. **ATE**: ate, date, fate, great, late, state, slate, straight, wait, weight, abate, donate

8. **EEM**: beam, cream, dream, gleam, steam, scheme, seem, stream, team, theme, esteem, redeem

A CEO of a pharmaceutical company, in speaking to his researchers on their search for new cures, said this:

> There is no <u>dream</u> beyond reach when we have in place here at Bristol-Myers the right <u>team</u>.

9. **AIN**: gain, pain, plain, reign, stain, strain, wane, vein, attain, retain, regain, explain, remain, sustain

Perhaps you can adopt this line of Adlai Stevenson's:

> There are no <u>gains</u> without <u>pains</u>.

Play around with any of the sounds in the Rhyming Nine, and you can come up with your own ringing line. Remember you need only one for a talk. Make it one that defines the problem or reinforces the solution.

The Echo Effect

Echo is the repetition of a word or a phrase. Kennedy's most quoted line is this one from his inaugural:

> Ask not what your country can do for you, but rather what you can do for your country.

Franklin Roosevelt's most famous line also came from his first inaugural, and it, too, features the echo effect:

> The only thing we have to fear is fear itself.

Lincoln's closing words of the Gettysburg Address also exploit the "echo" principle:

. . . that government of the people, by the people, and for the people shall not perish from the earth.

Two of President Reagan's most quoted statements were "echo" lines as well.

Government is not the solution to the problem; government is the problem.

and

The federal government did not create the states; the states created the federal government.

Some of Winston Churchill's most memorable lines employ the "echo" technique. Here are a few of them:

If you destroy a free market, you create a black market.

A fanatic is one who won't change his mind and won't change the subject.

We shape our dwellings and afterward our dwellings shape us.

All wisdom is not new wisdom.

Life is sensation; sensation is life.

The further backward we can look, the further forward we can see.

When France fell, Churchill manifested his defiance in the Dunkirk address, using this famous "echo" line:

We shall fight on the beaches, we shall fight on the landing grounds, we shall fight in the streets, we shall fight in the hills, we shall never surrender.

Richard Nixon etched this echoing epigram in his last book:

Always be prepared to negotiate, but never negotiate without being prepared.

In an 1890 speech to a convention of women in San Francisco, Susan B. Anthony warned her audience with this echoing statement:

Women must not depend on the protection of a man, but must be taught to protect herself.

CEOs as well as politicians create memorable lines through the echo technique. During World War II, Henry Ford told his employees at Dearborn:

It's not the employer who pays wages; he only handles the money; it's the product that pays the wages.

William F. Buckley Jr., the conservative columnist, used the "echo" technique to coin this aphorism:

The trouble with socialism is socialism— the trouble with capitalism is capitalists.

> **CEOs AS WELL AS POLITICIANS CREATE MEMORABLE LINES THROUGH THE ECHO TECHNIQUE.**

In minting your own "zinger," you have three ways to work the echo ploy:

1. *Repeat a word in the second phrase that you used in the first.*

Benjamin Franklin, for example, wrote these echo lines in his *Almanac:*

God helps those that help themselves.

One woman top executive in a cosmetic line company told her people this:

There is no future in any job. The future lies in you who have the job.

2. *Repeat the noun.*

Note how Churchill repeats victory in his first speech as prime minister.

What is our aim? I answer in one word. Victory—victory at all costs, victory is spite of all terror, victory however long and hard the road may be, for without victory there is no survival.

Churchill also used a repetitive preposition for the echo effect before a joint session of the U.S. Congress in 1941 when he proclaimed:

We have not journeyed across the oceans, across the prairies, across the mountains because we are made of sugar candy.

A head of a pharmaceuticals firm in a speech to his stockholders borrowed from Churchill when he said this:

You ask what is our plan. I'd answer in one word. Research for cures to control diabetes, research for formulas that do cut high blood pressure, research for medicine to reduce cholesterol.

3. *Repeat the verb.*

A soft drink executive borrowed from Churchill's Dunkirk address when he told his company what they were going to do to defeat their biggest competitor:

We will outsell them in Detroit. We will outsell them in Chicago, we will outsell them in Milwaukee, we will outsell them in Minneapolis [and he paused] and we won't take no for an answer.

The echo line that etches deepest in the memory is also the hardest to craft. That is the "phrase reversal." In his *Almanac*, Benjamin Franklin coined this aphorism:

Eat to live, don't live to eat.

At a conference I heard a hotel executive compare the decline of Howard Johnson in the 1960s with the rise of Marriott. Howard Johnson had not adapted to the changing needs of the travel inn industry. The executive summed it up this way:

> It's not that they planned to fail, but that they failed to plan.

Attorney General Robert Kennedy used to repeat to his staff this advice that his father, Joe Kennedy, used to drum into his sons:

> When the going gets tough, the tough get going.

At a staff meeting, the top executive of a resort chain told staff members this:

> A job is not just something you hold down. It does not serve to work if you don't work to serve.

A head of a sales force told his manufacturers' representatives this:

> All you need to know is to know his needs.

Alliterate and Activate

The fourth letter of C-R-E-A-M represents A*lliteration*, another old practiced verbal trick. By the way, consonants are better for alliteration than vowels. And the best of the consonants is "P." (Remember the nursery verse "Peter Piper Picked a Peck of Pickled Peppers"?)

Churchill once framed his secret of speaking in a series of P's.

> Vary the pose and vary the pitch and don't forget the pause.

Also using P's, Oregon governor Mark Hatfield, in his nomination speech of Richard Nixon in 1960, proclaimed:

> From Caracas to the Kremlin, he has been a pilgrim for peace and a pioneer for progress.

Listen to these words of John Kennedy's inaugural, featuring B's as well as P's:

That we shall pay any price, bear any burden . . .

Read again Martin Luther King's most quoted sentence in his 1963 address at the Lincoln Memorial, and note the alliteration of C's:

I have a dream that my four little children will one day live in a nation where they will be judged not by the color of their skin but by the content of their character.

In a similar appeal for tolerance, White House speechwriter Dick Goodwin coined this catchy line for President Johnson:

The world has narrowed into a neighborhood before it has broadened into a brotherhood.

I once heard a CEO explain his role at a company meeting in this way:

Do you know the role of a CEO? The executive exists to make exceptions to the general rules.

Alliteration Isn't Arduous

Alliteration isn't arduous. All you need is a $5.95 *Oxford Essential Thesaurus.*

Suppose you want to stress the idea that if you don't anticipate a customer's needs you're not going to sell your product.

Well you look up "anticipate" and find "sense" listed as a synonym. So you might rephrase your line this way:

If you don't sense a customer's needs, you won't sell your product.

Let's say you want to underscore the importance of driving down costs. To cut costs is to increase profits. You look up synonyms and try them out. "To cut costs is to swell sales"? No, that doesn't work. Then you hit on "produce" and write this:

The secret to producing profits is cutting costs.

A department store executive wanted to come up with a snappy punch line for her women's line buyers about really examining the goods closely instead of taking at face value the words in the wholesaler's pitch.

I worked with her and we played with the words "examine" and "look." Under "look" we found "eye." Immediately the word "ear" jumped into my mind as its comparison. Finally we devised this line.

> ALLITERATION ISN'T ARDUOUS. ALL YOU NEED IS A $5.95 *OXFORD ESSENTIAL THESAURUS.*

When you go to buy, rely not on your ear but on your eye!

The Metaphor Method

The last letter of the C-R-E-A-M acronym represents *Metaphor.* Aristotle once wrote:

The highest line of the poet is sometimes the hardest to imagine.

That's what imagery is—the fruit of your imagination.

Churchill had a method for jumpstarting his search for the right metaphor. He would say to himself, "Let's take a hike." And, like the psalmist-shepherd David, he would conjure up in his mind all the images of nature: rock, tree, stream, grass, pasture, path, hill, bush, mountain, flower.

Possibly that is how he coined the phrase "parley at the summit" (that is, summit conference), a phrase that, like "iron curtain," embedded itself permanently in the language of diplomacy.

Or Churchill would jumpstart his imagination by mentally going to the zoo, where he would picture the different beasts and birds. For Churchill the reptiles were the Nazis. This technique led to results such as this one:

An appeaser is one who feeds the crocodile, hoping it will eat him last.

And to this one about Nazi propaganda:

Like the boa constrictor, they first befoul their prey with their venom before engorging it.

Britain, on the other hand, was Churchill's "lion." Here's one of his lines using this metaphor:

We have no assurance that anyone else is going to keep the British Lion as a pet.

"Blood, Toil, Tears, and Sweat"

Other metaphors draw from body fluids: witness Churchill's "blood, toil, tears, and sweat."

General George Patton once used this line that seemed to borrow Churchill's imagery:

A pint of sweat will save a gallon of blood.

Let's turn again from politics to business. I read in the *Wall Street Journal* these words of a furniture manufacturer relating how they had overcome their wood supply problem:

What was a rivulet is now a river.

An auto industry head, in referring to the flaws of its competitors in the mid-size sedan market, said this:

The Bible asks, "Can the leopard change his spots?" Well, that particular car has not removed its spots or flaws.

A company head told his sales force:

Selling is simple—headwork plus legwork.

House and Home

Sometimes the familiar, everyday routines—household chores, shopping trips, or gardening tasks—suggest apt analogies. For example, President Roosevelt, in supporting the Lend Lease Act in 1940, made this statement:

> Who would not lend a hose to a neighbor whose house is burning down?

I used the following analogy of lawn mowing to explain the art of negotiation for President Nixon:

> It is like mowing a lawn. You first start at the outer edges and move to the center. With the Soviets, we will work out agreements on fishing rights in the Bering Sea before we get to the central core issue of missiles.

It is as easy as pie to cook up a Power Line. First, ask yourself: What is the gist of the "central" idea I want to get across? Write it out and play with it. Like Churchill, "go to the zoo" or "take a hike." Or, like Roosevelt, think of everyday things and tasks around the house. Or, like JFK, look at the Rhyming Nine. Find a synonym for alliteration as Ted Sorensen did for Kennedy.

> **SOMETIMES THE FAMILIAR, EVERYDAY ROUTINES—HOUSEHOLD CHORES, SHOPPING TRIPS, OR GARDENING TASKS—SUGGEST APT ANALOGIES.**

Remember, though, you only need one Power Line for your talk or presentation—your audience is unlikely to remember more than one line from your talk. Don't overuse these techniques, or they'll lose their effectiveness.

15

Power Question

This momentous question is like a fireball in the night.
—THOMAS JEFFERSON

For most of the presidential race during campaign year 1980, President Jimmy Carter was ahead of Governor Ronald Reagan. The Carter people had hoped that Reagan would defeat Bush in the Republican primaries. Reagan was thought to be easily beatable—too right wing and too lightweight. For most of the year, their predictions appeared correct, but by October the race was close. Then, during a TV debate in Philadelphia, Governor Reagan posed this question to the audience:

> Do you feel better off today than you did four years ago? Then vote for President Carter; but if you don't, vote for me.

The Momentous Question

From that moment on, the Carter campaign disintegrated. Reagan won in a massive victory. Sometimes the rightly phrased question packs the electric brightness and power of a lightning strike. Hone the thrust of your argument into one Power Question.

Some of Jesus Christ's most trenchant teachings are phrased in the form of a question. One of the most cited is this one:

> For what does a man profit if he shall gain the whole world but lose his soul?

He asked many other questions to get his listeners to think. To inspirit wavering followers, Jesus asked:

> Why are ye fearful, O ye of little faith?

Regarding love of your fellow man, Jesus asked:

> What man is there, who if his son asked for bread, would give him a stone?

Then in another of his parables, he poses this question:

> Which of you intending to build a tower does not sit down first to count the cost?

A question forces the listener to react, whereas a declarative sentence does not. A question can compel a listener to answer, even if in his or her own mind.

Abraham Lincoln defended his opposition to the Kansas-Nebraska proposal to let new territories choose if they wanted to have slaves by framing this question:

> Is not conservatism adherence to the old and tried instead of the new and untried?

The Question as a Quip

In one of his debates against Stephen Douglas, Lincoln wielded his wit with a Power Question. When the Democratic senator labeled him "two-faced," Lincoln replied:

> If God gave me two faces, would I be wearing this one?

In cross-examinations of witnesses, an iron-clad rule is to never ask a question if you are not sure of the answer. My father used to tell me of his experience representing an indigent in 1930:

> A homeless man had broken into a chicken coop, eaten one chicken, and then spent the night in the henhouse as shelter from a cold rain.
>
> The local district attorney had charged the vagrant with burglary, larceny, trespassing, and breaking and entering.
>
> On the stand, the prosecutor asked the accused, "Have you ever served in prison?"
>
> The man nodded.
>
> "Where?"
>
> The grizzled defendant answered, "Andersonville, Georgia."
> Andersonville, as most people knew, was the "Buchenwald" of the Civil War.
>
> My father, in his appeal to the jury, stated: "Don't you think that old man has served enough time in prison?"

My father knew what the answer would be to this question, and his indigent client was acquitted.

Using a Series of Questions

At the 1960 Republican convention, I heard the GOP keynoter, Minnesota Congressman Dr. Walter Judd, a former preacher and missionary, deliver a series of questions:

> Was it under Republican administration that seventy million people in Eastern Europe lost their freedom to Soviet Tyranny?
>
> Was it under Republican administration that the billions of Chinese were enslaved under a Communist dictator?

The audience roared back "No" to each of four questions Judd asked. Twenty-two years later, Judd told me that the text he had drafted read this way: "It was not under a Republican administration . . . ," but the veteran orator decided to turn each declarative statement into a Power Question.

> **NEVER ASK A QUESTION IF YOU ARE NOT SURE OF THE ANSWER.**

Rhetorical Power

Not all Power Questions demand answers of "yes" or "no"—even if unvoiced. Sometimes rhetorical questions—those to which no answer is expected—are posed as a speech device to motivate listeners to get involved.

In 1950, a Labour Party minister boasted about the good shape of British society under the socialist government and cited the increase in births and population to reinforce his argument. Churchill interrupted his opponent by asking this Power Question:

> Wouldn't the Honorable Gentleman agree that the last statistic on the birth rate is not due to socialism but private enterprise?

Of course, even when is is no reply, the answer may be assumed.

Susan B. Anthony made this Power Question the thrust of one of her most noted addresses:

> The only question left to be settled now is this: Are women persons?

At the midpoint of the baseball season, a business manager of a team whose pennant hopes of the spring had withered by July pondered the big-ticket payroll cost of his star pitcher. At the front office he posed this question:

> If we can't make it to the playoffs with him this year, shouldn't we trade him now for the players we need next year to be in contention?"

It was the Roman senator Cicero who made the rhetorical question an oratorical device later mastered by American orators Daniel Webster, Henry Clay, and John Calhoun.

In his attack on the corrupt "Cataline," Cicero asked:

How long, how long, O' Cataline, will you continue to abuse our patience?

The apostle Paul also used this device. One of his most quoted lines is this rhetorical question:

If the trumpet sounds an uncertain note, who shall prepare for battle?

The head of a huge food and home products conglomerate warned in a board meeting about of one of its salad dressing products.

How long are we going to throw money at this losing affiliate company in a declining sales market?

Master of Rhetoric

In December 1941, just after Pearl Harbor, Churchill was invited to address a joint session of Congress. After reciting "a litany of the outrages," he stated:

The Japanese have committed against us at Pearl Harbor, in the Pacific Islands, in the Philippines, in Malay . . . it becomes difficult to reconcile Japanese action with prudence or sanity.

Then he paused and delivered this rhetorical question:

What kind of people do they think we are?

The congressmen and senators rose to their feet and reacted with thunderous waves of applause for five minutes.

The rhetorical question delivered by Churchill at the U.S. Capitol is the Power Question at its greatest. Churchill thought that using such a rhetorical question once in a talk was enough, and that the question should be plain and blunt.

So, if you want to wake up an audience, wield a Power Question as Churchill did. Keep it to a single line, and keep it simple.

SOMETIMES RHETORICAL QUESTIONS—THOSE TO WHICH NO ANSWER IS EXPECTED—ARE POSED AS A SPEECH DEVICE TO MOTIVATE LISTENERS TO GET INVOLVED.

16

Power Word

The very word is like a bell.
—JOHN KEATS

In any talk or presentation, you may want to stress or emphasize one word. You don't do that by shouting it out. You do it most effectively by adding a little pause before uttering it.

My mother used to listen to Edward Murrow's radio reports from wartime Britain. As a six-year-old, I listened along with her and can still hear his portentous opening:

This [pause] is London.

After the war, his nightly report began:

This [pause] is the news.

A *New Yorker* magazine profile on Murrow stated:

On Judgment Day one can imagine a voice sounding like Murrow which would intone "This [pause] is the Lord."

In the article the writer wrote how Murrow learned the secret of pausing before a key word from his high school drama teacher in the state of Washington, where he grew up. The pause, said Murrow, focused attention on the word or phrase to follow.

Folksy radio commentator Paul Harvey ends his commentary similarly:

[pause] . . . Good day.

Winston Churchill had a different trick. Churchill was a stutterer. He worked out a way to mask his involuntary stammer by inserting a deliberate stutter. If he had a key word that he wanted to engrave in his listeners' minds, he found that using a contrived stutter made him less worried or self-conscious of his unintended stutter. Eventually, with the help of this device, Churchill's involuntary stutter began to disappear.

> CHURCHILL WOULD INTRODUCE COMPELLING OR UNUSUAL WORDS WITH A DELIBERATE STUTTERING PAUSE.

Introducing Power Words

Churchill would introduce compelling or unusual words with a deliberate stuttering pause. When he spoke in 1941 of the U.S. Lend-Lease Program, he said:

This act is a most [stutter-pause] unsordid act.

Churchill created a word that is unrecorded anywhere else when he put a negative prefix on "sordid."

Churchill employed another word that is rarely found: "benignant," the antonym of the more common word "malignant." Here it is, as Churchill used it in a speech:

Let the growing Anglo-American relationship roll on like the Mississippi—increasingly powerful and [stuttering pause] benignant.

If you listen to a taped recording of a Churchill radio address in 1943, you will hear his stutter-pause as he coined a new word by appropriating the name of notorious Norwegian collaborator Vidkun Quisling:

These vile [stutter-pause] quislings in our midst will use the new word which will carry the scorn of mankind down the centuries.

In his early years in the House of Commons, Churchill coined this comical euphemism for a lie.

Perhaps I have been guilty of a [stammer-pause] terminological inexactitude.

Introducing Power Phrases

Pregnant pauses can turn even familiar words or phrases into compelling communication. Churchill poignantly paused to introduce this allusion to Henry V's lines in Shakespeare's play of that name:

Let us, therefore, brace ourselves to our duties and so bear ourselves to our duties that if the British Empire and its Commonwealths last for a thousand years, they will say "This was [stuttering pause] our finest hour."

Franklin Roosevelt also knew the power of the strategic pause to introduce an unusual word. In his radio address after Pearl Harbor, he selected an arresting word to describe the unprovoked attack.

Yesterday, December 7th, a date which will live in [pause] infamy, Pearl Harbor was suddenly and deliberately attacked . . .

Roosevelt might have chosen an alliterative word, such as "disgrace," but he used "infamy," a word not otherwise found in *Bartlett's Familiar Quotations.* "Infamy," Roosevelt figured, would be a word that would capture the next morning's headlines, and it did.

Roosevelt coined another of his magnificent phrases in December 1940, before we entered the war:

We must be [pause] the great arsenal of democracy.

When I was attending a British public school in 1953, I had the role of the second gentleman in *Henry VIII,* the last play that Shakespeare wrote. Emlyn Williams, the Welsh actor and playwright who crossed America some years later reading passages from Charles Dickens in a one-man show, came to coach us in our acting. His son also had a role in this performance.

In every line an actor delivers, said Williams, you'll find one word that carries the thrust of the statement. You can discover that word if you mumble

> PREGNANT PAUSES CAN TURN EVEN FAMILIAR WORDS OR PHRASES INTO COMPELLING COMMUNICATION.

every other word of the line but clearly pronounce that key word. Pause before offering that word.

One of my lines referred to Cardinal Wolsey. The key word was "perniciously," and Emlyn Williams told me I had to pause before that word. That pause made me roll over the syllables in my mouth to suggest hate and violence toward the Cardinal.

> All the Commons hate him [pause] perniciously and wished him ten fathoms deep.

Twenty-five years later Sir John Gielgud, who in my mind was the greatest Shakespearean actor of the past century, told me essentially the same thing:

> James, Larry [Olivier] approaches characters by working out his face and body movements first—outside to the inner. I start with the language. I identify certain words of the central character—Hamlet, Prospero, Richard II—and see a word that is a clue to his character, and I make sure the audience can savor those core words.

General MacArthur had the skills of an orator and the talents of an actor. He knew how to set up a Power Word, as was evident in 1942 when he left Corregidor in the Philippines for Australia and pronounced this memorable line:

> I shall [pause] return.

He used that famous pause again when he spoke to a joint session of Congress in 1951 after he was dismissed by Truman. MacArthur intoned:

There is no substitute for [pause] victory.

Actors know the effect of the pause in keying a word in every line. Political leaders who have acting skills—such as Churchill, Roosevelt, and Reagan—might choose to emphasize two or three words in a talk. But if you're an executive, limit yourself to one "impact" word per talk or statement.

Adjective Assassination

In the 1976 presidential campaign, when I was working as a speechwriter for President Ford, the Republican headquarters discerned reservations about Governor Carter, particularly from Northern Democrats. As a result, states such as Connecticut and New Jersey were up for grabs. Their suspicions about Carter had something to do with his being "born again," his sighting of a UFO, and his "lust in my heart" interview in *Playboy* magazine.

> IF YOU'RE AN EXECUTIVE, LIMIT YOURSELF TO ONE "IMPACT" WORD PER TALK OR STATEMENT.

Ford told a few of us that some of his Democratic friends from Capitol Hill days—even though they were supporting their party standard bearer—confided that there was something "odd" about Carter, something they couldn't quite put their finger on. They admitted they felt more comfortable with Ford.

We seized on "odd" as a word that even many Democrats believed applied to Carter. In a political gambit called "adjective assassination," we featured the adjective "odd" and its synonyms—bizarre, strange, weird—when crafting comments about Governor Carter's actions or statements. These would be incorporated into Ford's messages from the Rose Garden that were designed to capture the evening TV news headlines. Ford was coached—with marginal success—to pause for the key word. Here are a few examples:

> Frankly, we find that statement by Governor Carter on the defense policy rather [pause] odd considering . . .

> We think his choice of this foreign relations advisor [pause] bizarre when you think that he said the Cold War had been exaggerated.

> Isn't it a little bit [pause] strange, his statement yesterday on integrated public housing, when he used the phrase "ethnic purity" in the primary. . . .

We weren't actually calling Jimmy Carter himself "odd," but that was the impression we, not too subtly, were trying to convey.

In every statement you make—whether an announcement or brief remarks introducing a new product—identify a key word. You might, for example, use the word "constructive" to explain negotiations or "revolutionary" to describe a software innovation.

> IN EVERY STATEMENT YOU MAKE—WHETHER AN ANNOUNCEMENT OR BRIEF REMARKS INTRODUCING A NEW PRODUCT—IDENTIFY A KEY WORD.

Turn a key word into a Power Word: reinforce it the way Roosevelt did—with a strategic pause.

17

Power Active

Divest oneself of passivity.
—Dr. Martin Luther King

In 1904 General Eisenhower asked Winston Churchill to look over a speech he had drafted. Churchill read it and said, "Dwight, it has too many passives and too many zeds."

"Zed" is what the British say for the letter we call "zee," and Churchill was referring to the verbs "systemize," "prioritize," and "finalize" in Eisenhower's text. Churchill would say "end" or "finish" instead of "finalize", but his main complaint was Ike's use of the passive voice. That's when the true subject—the doer of the action—either is not in the sentence at all or is relegated to object of a preposition.

Passive Is Pale

Look over these four lines:

1. "When liberty is given up to purchase a little temporary safety, then neither liberty nor safety is deserved.
2. "Liberty is granted only to those who love it."
3. "An inevitable victory will be obtained."

4. "Eighty-seven years ago a new government was established."

Get the point?

For the first example, the actual words of Benjamin Franklin read:

They that give up essential liberty to purchase a little temporary safety, deserve neither liberty nor safety.

The second example was a corruption of Daniel Webster's famous line:

God grants liberty to those who love it.

The third example turns a line from President Franklin Roosevelt's "day of infamy" address after Pearl Harbor to passive. The real version reads:

We shall gain the inevitable triumph.

The fourth example makes the opening sentence of the Gettysburg Address sound insipid—not only because "fourscore and seven" was changed but also because "our fathers brought forth upon this continent" was turned around to the passive voice. The sentence no longer includes "our fathers"—those responsible for bringing forth our new nation.

We do not need to make up examples, however. In February 1942, at a time when America faced the threat of bombing by both the Germans and the Japanese, an official from the General Services Administration presented Franklin Roosevelt with a copy of a notice that would be placed in every room of every government office across the land. The bureaucrat read this aloud to the president:

> PASSIVE VOICE IS WHEN THE TRUE SUBJECT—THE DOER OF THE ACTION— EITHER IS NOT IN THE SENTENCE AT ALL OR IS RELEGATED TO OBJECT OF A PREPOSITION.

IT IS OBLIGATORY THAT ALL
ILLUMINATION BE EXTINGUISHED
BEFORE THE PREMISES ARE
VACATED.

Roosevelt, known for his clear communication, wryly replied,

Why the hell can't you say "Put out the lights when you leave"?

Put Passives Down the Rathole

In June 1940, President Roosevelt, along with his aide and friend, Harry Hopkins, tuned in to hear Prime Minister Winston Churchill's speech on the fall of France, after which Britain stood alone in Europe against the Nazi invaders.

In the residential quarters on the second floor of the White House, the president and Hopkins heard Churchill say this:

We shall fight them on the beaches, we shall fight them on the landing grounds, we shall fight them in the streets and in the hills. We shall never surrender.

Roosevelt turned to Hopkins and said:

Well, Harry, as long as that old bastard's in charge, Britain will never surrender. It's not like putting money down the rathole as in France.

Churchill's words had left no doubt that England was willing to take responsibility. Because of that speech, a neutral United States dispatched arms and weaponry to a beleaguered Britain.

In May 1940, when Prime Minister Neville Chamberlain resigned, a coalition of three parties replaced the Conservative government. The choice was between Churchill and Labour leader Clement Attlee.

Churchill once described Attlee as "a modest man with much to be modest about." A Churchill aide once came up with this passive version of how Attlee would have declared his resolve:

> It is imperative that the defenses of the coastal perimeter should be maintained.

Do you think that if Roosevelt had heard British determination expressed in that "passive" voice, he would have broken his nation's neutrality to send destroyers as well as supplies in merchant ships?

Webster's Dictionary defines the passive voice with this:

> In grammar indicating that the subject is the receiver (object) of the action the verb denotes (e.g. the tree was struck by lightning).

But "passive" is also defined as "unresisting mentally or physically, inactive, lifeless, unenthusiastic."

Passive Voice, Passive Mind

There is good reason this form of grammatical construction is called the passive voice, as verbal constructions employing the passive voice too often suggest the passive state of mind that is represented by the other definition of "passive."

Was it unfair for Churchill's aide to ascribe to Attlee what *he might have said?* Well, read what Deputy Prime Minister Clement Attlee actually said about social problems after the war. He told an International Labor Conference this:

> **VERBAL CONSTRUCTIONS EMPLOYING THE PASSIVE VOICE TOO OFTEN SUGGEST THE PASSIVE STATE OF MIND.**

> We are determined that economic questions and questions of the universal improvement of living and nutrition shall not be neglected after the last war owing to the preoccupation with political problems.

That kind of speaking would drive Sominex out of business!

Whabby, Flabby

In wartime London, some ranking members of Churchill's own cabinet spoke in "bureaucratese." One was the education minister, Richard Austen Butler, who was also called "Rab" for his initials.

Politicians called Butler "Wab" behind his back, because he pronounced the letter "R" as a "W," much as when Elmer Fudd calls Bugs Bunny "a wascal."

One afternoon Churchill's presence was required while "Wab" Butler delivered a turgid and convoluted address explaining his plan for the restructuring of state schools.

The impatient prime minister, following along on the handed-out text of Butler's talk, began to underline all the auxiliaries in the "to be" family of words that precede the passive verb construction.

<u>Were</u> established
<u>Have been</u> propounded
<u>Are</u> constructed
<u>Be</u> safeguarded

Then Churchill wrote this in the margin:

Whab is flabby and blabby.

Well, when you finish writing your first draft of a statement or a talk, check it for "Whabby" words, such as these:

Were,
Have, had
Are, is
Be, been

The acronym "WHAB" can help you find words that sound a warning bell for potential overuse of the passive.

Exculpatory Voice (or "Cover-Your-Ass Passive")

Churchill called the passive voice the "exculpatory voice." The passive is the verbal tool of those who want to exonerate themselves. Here are a few examples:

Certain misstatements were made.

(Not "We lied.")

Reductions in personnel may be instituted.

(Not "We are going to fire a lot of employees.")

Certain errors in judgment were made.

(Not "We goofed.")

The passive is for the "cover-your-ass" types. But the active voice is for the take-charge leaders. The passive is not the voice of a leader. The passive is the voice of the bureaucrat who wants to duck responsibility. He or she might say this:

The policy will be implemented . . .

The leader, on the other hand, would say this:

Let's do it!

Passives rob a talk of life and action. They turn the vibrant words of punchy conversation into the pale gray of "governmentese."

> **THE PASSIVE IS FOR THE "COVER-YOUR-ASS" TYPES. BUT THE ACTIVE VOICE IS FOR THE TAKE-CHARGE LEADERS.**

The passive voice construction is the turtle of grammar. The slow and plodding turtle is distinguished by his ability to retract his head and hide it underneath his shell. The passive compared to the active voice is not only more cumbersome but also deprives the listener of information about the actor or perpetrator of the action. Take this sentence:

The jobs will be terminated by December 1.

What the listener really wants to know is *who is responsible* for the firings, a detail that a weakling corporate executive would prefer to hide.

Some corporate executives like the passive because it uses convoluted phrasing that they think seems more authoritative because it sounds complex. They're wrong. The active voice provides force to your speech, whereas the passive voice sounds spineless and deadens your delivery.

So toss out the tendentious turtles and pick up your pace.

Try to find a passive verb construction in Napoleon's address to his troops before the Italians. Try to spot one in Susan B. Anthony's speech in 1873 to a women's rights group in Seneca. Try to discover one in Franklin Roosevelt's first inaugural address in 1933.

> THE ACTIVE VOICE PROVIDES FORCE TO YOUR SPEECH, WHEREAS THE PASSIVE VOICE SOUNDS SPINELESS AND DEADENS YOUR DELIVERY.

Finally, check out Lincoln's Gettysburg Address. You'll find no "passives" there, either.

So use a Power Active and empower your delivery. Don't be a "whabby" wimp. Be like Churchill, and charge up your presentation with some energy.

18

Power Dollar

A still soliciting eye
—William Shakespeare

If Ronald Reagan was the "Great American Communicator," Benjamin Franklin was the "Great Persuader."

The Great Persuader

When the largest American colony was deadlocked over the vote for the Declaration of Independence, Benjamin Franklin persuaded John Morton to vote for the resolution even though it would probably guarantee his defeat from his district by telling Morton:

> You will be remembered in history as a Signer.

Morton was defeated, as Franklin had predicted, but Pennsylvania got its vote for freedom.

Then, as minister to France, Franklin persuaded King Louis XVI to put up 300,000 francs to keep George Washington's Continental Army in the field.

After the war Franklin persuaded a reluctant Great Britain to sign the Treaty of Paris, which recognized the new United States and gave us all the land from the

Appalachians to the Mississippi. There was little advantage for Britain in signing the treaty. Britain could have just as easily left the independent colonies in limbo.

At the Constitutional Convention, Franklin persuaded the delegates to accept the "two-house" compromise, which entailed having both a House, based on population, and a Senate, with two representatives from each state.

This Great Persuader was also the first superb fundraiser. He knew how to part money from purses and wallets. Franklin raised the dollars for the first public library in America. Franklin found the donors for the first hospital in America. Franklin secured the funding for the first college in Philadelphia (now the University of Pennsylvania). Franklin formed the first foundation in America. In fact, Franklin even invented the idea of "matching gifts" in fund-raising drives.

Franklin began developing his formula for raising capital at the age of nineteen, when he was an apprentice printer in Philadelphia. He didn't have any local network of family or friends because he had been born in Boston, so he needed something to set him apart from other printers in Philadelphia. This is how he did just that:

Franklin was aware that William Keith, the governor of Pennsylvania, usually took his supper at about five o'clock at City Tavern. So Franklin approached Governor Keith's table at about six o'clock, when he was finishing up with his pie and port.

"Your Excellency," said Franklin, "you are the governor of Pennsylvania, and our capital city, Philadelphia, is the biggest city—except of course for London—in the entire British Empire of His Majesty, George II. Your statutes, laws, proclamations, and declarations need to look handsome and elegant on the printed page in a style worthy of your exalted rank."

The governor nodded appreciatively. "Well, what do your propose, lad?"

"Give me money for sea passage to London, and I will find the best printing press in the world and buy it, my lord."

Franklin got the ticket. True, the governor never sent him passage for return, but while he was in London for four years, Franklin mastered the latest techniques in printing. When he came back to Philadelphia, he soon became the city's top printer.

Consider this: Franklin, still a teenager, dared to confront the most powerful personage in Philadelphia, Governor William Keith, and ask him for money.

We can describe the Franklin formula for fund-raising with these four words that begin with "D":

Defiance
Design
Donation
Duel

Defiance: Your Ticket to Treasure

"Defiance" is a strong word. It suggests a presumptuous, audacious, or even cocky attitude. That's right—cocky!

The first step in fund-raising is psychological. Franklin said that you must psyche yourself into believing that you are doing this investor a favor. You are giving him the chance to be a winning entrepreneur. You are going to make him a bundle! You are giving him a map to the pot at the end of the rainbow!

> WE CAN DESCRIBE THE FRANKLIN FORMULA FOR FUND-RAISING WITH THESE FOUR WORDS THAT BEGIN WITH "D": DEFIANCE, DESIGN, DONATION, DUEL.

Keep reminding yourself that you are not a teenager asking your dad to buy you a car or begging for more allowance or a prom dress. You're going in as an equal— seller to buyer. You are offering the opportunity of a big bonanza. In a sense, you're selling the potential investor a ticket to treasure.

So don't be a supplicator on bended knee. Stride in with a purposeful gait. Look him (or her) right in the eyes, and say:

Mr. (or Ms.) Moneybags, I'd like to take a moment of your time and talk about being part of a great market opportunity.

When Franklin went to Governor Keith's table, it wasn't like asking his father, the candlestick maker, if he could borrow the family horse for a trip to see a young damsel on the other side of Boston. He was offering a way to make the governor look good—with new eye-catching proclamations.

Design: Paint a Picture

The next "D" is for *Design.* Franklin said you must paint a picture of that new product. When Franklin invented the lightning rod, he described to investors how the rod would protect houses from being struck by lightning by deflecting a lightning strike.

Later in his career, Franklin invented bifocals. Then he showed interested backers how he could identify the different trees outside his window yet still look down and read a book with the same pair of spectacles.

Franklin knew investors would not invest their dollars in something intangible. They wouldn't back him just because he had a reputation for being a clever man. They had to picture how the new product would work. Donors like to visualize what they are investing in.

You must practice your presentation until your excitement comes through. Then you can show the investor the plan of the new resort or retirement community. Churchill once said this about drafting a presentation or a talk:

There is in the act of preparing that moment when you start caring.

Donors must see that *you* really care about the project before they will care.

Don't swamp those you wish to persuade with numbers. Sure, tell them what it's going to cost, but don't reel off a raft of numbers. Save these as answers to their questions about profits and yields.

Just pick one or two startling facts. For example, if your product relates to seniors, you might give the new numbers on retired people—how that population is getting larger because they're living longer.

Or, with a map, display the intersection of roads near a proposed shopping mall to show that it will be the most accessible place in the metropolitan area. Tell investors about the reduced risks but the probable profits in your venture.

> **DONORS MUST SEE THAT *YOU* REALLY CARE ABOUT THE PROJECT BEFORE THEY WILL CARE.**

Put passion in to your presentation. Put some romance in your recital. Tell the investor how he will be creating jobs, shaping history, and building tomorrow all while reaping big dividends and big profits.

Donation: Faint Heart Wins Not

The third "D" of fund-raising is for *Donation.* How much should you ask for? What is the amount that you are going to seek? Franklin said this about requesting donations:

> "What is the most you think you can ask for? Then *double* it! Don't base your request on how much he will give you but on how much you will need!

Franklin also invented the first home security device, which was nicknamed the "Philadelphia Busy Body." It consisted of a double set of mirrors—one mirror from the second story that caught an image of, say, a hallway, which was then picked up by another mirror on the first floor.

Franklin asked for $1,000, not just the $500 he needed to make the mirrors. He got what he asked for.

In another instance, he asked the French monarch for 500,000 francs, not just the 200,000 that was his original, arrived-at figure. He got 300,000 francs.

Know Your Number

Franklin also advised that you have a *specific* figure in mind. Don't say, "How much do you think you can invest?" That's a way of asking that's almost inviting rejection. Try a more confident, specific approach, such as this one:

> Ms. Donor, we are seeking one person to be the founding investor for a quarter of a million. We want you to be the founding investor.

Or say this:

> Mr. Fat Cat, we have in mind five original investors who will be the captains, so to speak, of this venture—each for $100,000. We are counting on you, Mr. Fat Cat, to be one of these captains.

Duel: High Noon at the O.K. Corral!

The fourth "D" is for *Duel.* In Franklin's day, dueling was still a way of settling disputes of honor. Although the practice was outlawed, authorities simply winked at the violators.

Franklin believed that turndowns happen because the asker speaks too soon after the request. Imagine that it is high noon at the O.K. corral and you must let your potential investor draw first. Wait until he answers before you say anything. The wait—not the asking—is the hardest part, but it's the sure-fire formula for fund-raising.

Say, for example, "Ms. Big Bucks, we want you to be the charter investor." Then pause and wait for her answer. Look her in the eye and wait. If you speak first after the request, you've lost her—perhaps forever. When you say something like, "We hope you will consider it" or "I'll call you back next week," you've stepped down from being an equal. You're back to being a teenager asking Dad for the car.

Wait; she may need time to figure out her cash-flow situation. With fixed eyes, stare straight into her eyes. Give her, as Shakespeare wrote, "that still soliciting eye."

Wait, wait, and wait some more—until her eyes blink. While waiting, stand like a statue—without a flicker of movement. Let her be the first to break the gaze and talk. It's like playing "chicken" with another driver on a one-lane road. Let the other driver make the first move to turn aside.

If she answers first, she almost never says no.

She might say, "Let me think about it" or "Let me get back to you." She might even say, "I'll go for fifty, not a hundred thousand."

By the way, if the prospective donor does say she'll call back in a week, don't stand by your telephone. Wait ten days or two weeks, and then call her at lunchtime— when she's not there!

She might not have thought of your visit and request during those ten days to two weeks. Many of us postpone a decision by putting it out of our minds. So, don't catch her unawares with a telephone call. If you ask for a sudden decision, it's likely to be a disappointing one for you. By leaving a phone message, you are gently reminding her.

On that rare occasion when the would-be donor does say no, you have at least taken her measure as an equal and won her respect. She will regard you as an equal player and remember you as an entrepreneur worth keeping an eye on.

Ask Your Prospect for Advice

People never mind being solicited for advice; in fact, they're usually pleased. When you talk with your prospective investor again, don't talk about money at first. Ask how she sees the idea—how she envisions such a project.

Once you have her giving advice, she's halfway committed to giving the money.

Finally, don't think a letter will take the place of a personal visit. Franklin gave this advice to John Paul Jones, who in 1777 was in Le Havre, France, waiting for the king of France to answer his request to be outfitted with some ships.

DON'T THINK A LETTER WILL TAKE THE PLACE OF A PERSONAL VISIT.

Before Franklin sailed back to Philadelphia from Le Havre, he left a French version of his book *Bon Homme Richard* (French for "Poor Richard") at Jones's office, with a bookmark flagging this saying:

Never try to ask by letter
To go yourself is far better

Captain Jones took the advice and went to Versailles. The king gave him three ships; he called the flagship *Le Bon Homme Richard.* And it was on the bridge of that ship that Jones would later say these well-known words:

I've just begun to fight.

So, when raising money, be defiant like John Paul Jones. Take the formula of Franklin—America's first self-made millionaire, the first big American success story. Remember, as Franklin did, that you are giving your prospective investors the opportunity of their lifetime.

Show them your design for the future, and boldly ask for a donation.

And don't forget Franklin's most important advice: Put into play the psychological weapon of the duel. After you ask, keep your mouth shut like a clam.

Use the Franklin formula and be a winning fundraiser too.

19

Power Button

Our words have wings
but fly not where we would.
—George Eliot

Now that you have worked up a dandy Power Line, you need to know how to turn it on. You have to light your line so it stands out like a neon sign.

Look, you put in some time to work for that zinger of a line. Don't you want to make sure it really registers? If you don't know the secret of turning on your Power Line, you won't turn on the audience.

Ready, Set, Listen

The Power Button says to the audience "Ready—Set—Listen" to set them up for the Power Line that follows.

When writing an article, you can italicize. You can underline. But how can you italicize or underline in a talk? Listeners cannot hear the underlining of a sentence.

A lot of you may use a highlighter pen to emphasize a significant line when you read a report or survey. Well, the Power Button phrase is your highlighter pen, illuminating the Power Line that follows.

When I served in the Ford White House, President Ford would invite a speechwriter to join him for a drink if a quotation from a speech made it into the *New York Times's* "Quotation of the Day" or the *Wall Street Journal's* "Notable and Quotable."

> THE POWER BUTTON PHRASE IS YOUR HIGHLIGHTER PEN, ILLUMINATING THE POWER LINE SENTENCE THAT FOLLOWS.

That was when I discovered the Power Button secret, crafting sentences that would signal to the listening journalists to be ready for the zinger I had inserted in President Ford's talk.

Once I wrote this Power Line:

> Perhaps we have not always lived up to our ideals, but then no country ever wrote higher ideals to live up to.

Then, to introduce my Power Line, I constructed this Power Button sentence:

> LET ME AGAIN SAY WHAT I ALWAYS TELL THOSE CRITICS OF AMERICA:

One top executive in the hotel business had a line he was fond of using:

> The science of business is the science of service.

So, for his Power Button, I crafted this preamble:

> THE SECRET IN HOTEL MANAGEMENT IS SIMPLE. IT CAN BE SUMMED UP THIS WAY: [pause] The science of business . . .

Light Up a Line Like a Neon Sign

Presidents Franklin Roosevelt and John Kennedy both used a Power Button to dramatize the phrases in their inaugural addresses that were to become the two most memorable inaugural lines of all time:

Here's FDR's, spoken in March 1933:

> LET ME AGAIN ASSERT MY FIRM BELIEF [pause] that the only
> thing we have to fear is fear itself.

Why did Roosevelt say "my firm belief"? Are we to think that he was wishy-washy about the other things he talked about in his inaugural address, that he didn't have solid convictions about them? That was FDR's sentence. It then flashed up his Power Line like an airplane writing in the sky.

How did John Kennedy introduce his most-quoted line?

> AND SO MY FELLOW AMERICANS: [pause] Ask not what your
> country can do for you—ask what you can do for your country.

Kennedy said this in the middle of his address to alert his audience so they would listen to his challenge. This was JFK's Power Button, his ignition switch to turn on his Power Line.

Switch on the Ignition with a Power Button

This tactic of setting up a Power Line has been used throughout the ages by successful orators. The Greeks had a word for this set-up line: *pronyche.* Demosthenes, the greatest Athenian orator, applied the technique, in 341 B.C., in warning his audience about Philip of Macedonia:

> IT IS A PARADOX AND TRUTH THAT I SHALL STATE [pause] what
> is the worst in the past that can be the best for the future?

Politicians throughout history have continued to use the set-up line to command the attention their Power Line deserves. Winston Churchill spotlighted his most famous phrase, in his first speech as prime minister, by pushing a Power Button.

> I WOULD SAY TO THE HOUSE AS I SAID TO THOSE WHO JOINED
> THIS GOVERNMENT [pause] I have nothing to offer but blood,
> toil, tears, and sweat.

In the Gettysburg Address, Abraham Lincoln introduced his closing peroration with this Power Button
phrase:

> THAT WE HERE HIGHLY RESOLVE: [pause] That these men shall
> not have died in vain, that this nation under God shall have a
> new birth of freedom, and that government of the people, by the
> people, and for the people shall not perish from the earth.

How did Patrick Henry, the Revolutionary era's greatest
orator, introduce his immortal words? Again, with a Power
Button:

> I KNOW NOT WHAT OTHERS SAY, BUT AS FOR ME, [pause] give
> me liberty or give me death.

Push Your Power Button

The most delivered speech in the early part of the twentieth century was the "Cross of Gold" speech by William
Jennings Bryan. His oration swept the Democratic convention in 1896 and caused the little-known thirty-eight-year-
old congressman to receive the presidential nomination. It
was so electric in its effect that he would give it hundreds
of times for the next fifteen years while on speech tours.
Incidentally, Bryan's "Cross of Gold" was the first speech
that was entirely recorded on a wax disc.

> WE WILL ANSWER THEIR DEMAND BY SAYING TO THEM: [pause]
> You shall not press down upon the brow of labor this crown of
> thorns, you shall not crucify mankind upon a cross of gold.

Bryan's contemporary Theodore Roosevelt also used a
Power Button phrase to introduce the memorable sentence that defined his philosophy of life:

> I PREACH TO YOU, MY FELLOW COUNTRYMEN: [pause] That our
> country calls not for the life of ease but the life of strenuous endeavor.

The Exception(al) Reagan

The great communicator Ronald Reagan is too little represented in the latest edition of *Bartlett's Familiar Quotations*. Some of his devotees may attribute this to the political predilections of the book's contemporary editors, but it may also be explained in part by Reagan's aversion to this rhetorical trick. His first inaugural address, which was drafted by Tony Dolan, carried this Power Line that employed the echo effect:

> If we love our country, why shouldn't we also love our countrymen.

While having drinks with Dolan at the Hay-Adams in Washington, I suggested this Power Button sentence:

> AND SO, MY FRIENDS, I SAY TO YOU [pause], if we love our country . . .

Dolan shook his head, saying, "The governor doesn't like that kind of thing. He thinks it sounds like Senator Claghorn." (Claghorn was a comical windbag politician on the Fred Allen radio show in the 1940s.) And it's true, if you lard your talks with phrases like "so, my fellow citizens," or "let me say to you," or "and so, ladies and gentlemen," you might sound like some state senator bloviating at a county fair.

Reagan had his own test for a talk. He would imagine the way he'd talk to his barber, Jack, in Santa Barbara. He liked language that you would use in talking at your kitchen table or over the back fence.

> REAGAN HAD HIS OWN TEST FOR A TALK. HE WOULD IMAGINE THE WAY HE'D TALK TO HIS BARBER, JACK, IN SANTA BARBARA.

Reagan had disdain for the crafted rhetoric that Ted Sorensen wrote for Kennedy. He would never have said, "And so my fellow Americans: Ask not what . . ." To Reagan, such phrasing sounded too pontifical

LIMIT YOURSELF TO
ONE POWER BUTTON IN
EACH TALK, AND THEN USE
IT ONLY TO SPOTLIGHT
A ZINGER LINE THAT
YOU WANT TO LEAVE A
BURNING HOLE IN YOUR
LISTENERS' EARS.

and pompous. So he didn't highlight some of his ringing lines, thereby sacrificing "quotability" for "credibility."

One Power Button Per Speech

I do not suggest that you overuse and overwork this Power Button device. Limit yourself to one Power Button in each talk, and then use it only to spotlight a zinger line that you want to leave a burning hole in your listeners' ears.

20

Power Closer

Great is the art of beginning,
but greater is the art of ending.
—HENRY WADSWORTH LONGFELLOW

In his 1960 presidential campaign, John Kennedy did a series of airport rallies across the country. On each tarmac, he would read the short talk prepared by his speechwriter, Ted Sorensen. Then at the end of the typed remarks, Kennedy might look down and see a drawing of a sun, which would trigger his ending:

> At the close of the constitutional convention the oldest delegate, Benjamin Franklin, was asked to be the first to sign. At the front of the chamber was the chair from which General Washington had presided. The chair back had the design of a sun low on the horizon. Franklin said, "There were days when I thought this picture of a sun low on the horizon was a setting sun, but I now know it's a rising sun—a new day for America, a new dawn for freedom."

Another image that Sorensen would sketch for Kennedy at the bottom of the typed remarks was the outline of a candle. The candle would prompt this closing:

In Hartford, Connecticut, one day in 1780, the skies at noon turned from blue to gray, and by midafternoon the city had darkened over so densely that, in that religious age, men fell on their knees and begged a final blessing before the end of the world descended. The Connecticut House of Delegates was in session. There was pandemonium, and many of the House were calling for adjournment. The Speaker of the House, Colonel Davenport, rose to his feet and then silenced the din with these words:

"The Day of Judgment is either at hand or it is not at hand. If it is not, there is no need for adjournment. If it is, I choose to be found by my God doing my duty. I entertain the motion, therefore, that candles be brought to enlighten this hall of democracy."

A Strong Last Impression

Like Kennedy, Churchill believed in a strong closer. In "The Scaffolding of Rhetoric," Churchill urged a dramatic closer. The ending, he argued, is the last impression the speaker leaves with an audience. Even if your talk has been flat, you can still leave the audience roused with a good closer. For such a strong ending, said Churchill, you have to appeal to the emotions—pride, hope, love, and, occasionally, fear.

Pride—pride in the company, pride in the community, pride in one's profession or occupation

Hope—a vision for the future, hope for tomorrow, new opportunities, expanded horizons

Love—love of family, love of country, love of God

Fear—the disaster that might happen if steps are not taken immediately

Scripture or Shakespeare

To deepen the emotional impact, Churchill would sometimes quote verse from Scripture or Shakespeare. Sometimes he would inject a personal experience. He did both in a radio talk appealing for aid from the United States:

The other day I received a letter from President Roosevelt in which was enclosed a poem by Longfellow that was written in his own hand.

Sail on, O Ship of State!
Sail on, Union, strong and great!
Humanity with all its doubts and fears,
And all its hopes for future years,
Is hanging breathless on thy fate!

When Churchill had finished reciting the verse, he looked up and said,

> FOR A STRONG ENDING, SAID CHURCHILL, YOU HAVE TO APPEAL TO THE EMOTIONS—PRIDE, HOPE, LOVE, AND, OCCASIONALLY, FEAR.

What is the answer that I shall give to America and President Roosevelt? Here it is:
"Give us the tools and we will finish the job."

On another occasion, Churchill delivered a short talk while visiting a bombed section of East London. He cited Scripture to create this effective closing:

We remember the story of the prophet Amos. The Lord called out to him, "Amos, what do you see?"
Amos replied, "I see a wall."
Then the Lord said, "What do you see beside the wall?"
And Amos replied, "I see a plumb line."
"Behold," said the Lord, "I am setting a plumb line to find out how straight the people of Israel stand."
Well, we have seen in the last days how strong and straight the people of East London have stood.

On the occasion of the fall of France, Churchill borrowed his closing from the Anglican Prayer Book.

Today is Trinity Sunday. Centuries ago words were written to be called and support the faithful servants of truth and justice. "Arm yourselves and be ye men of valor, and be in readiness for the conflict; for it is better for us to persist in battle than to look upon the outrage of our nation and altar. As the Will of God is in Heaven, even so let it be."

Reagan Magic

The Great Communicator, Ronald Reagan, also knew the magic of an emotional ending. Those who heard his short talk at the Kansas City convention of 1976, after he lost to Ford, remember their eyes moistening as he ended by telling his audience never to forget the vision.

When Governor John Winthrop in 1630 called together his Puritan passengers on the flagship *Arabella,* he delivered them the challenge of building the new colony. He told them: "We must always consider that we shall be a city upon a hill—the eyes of the people upon us."

In his inaugural address in 1981, President Reagan touched the heartstrings with this closer:

Under a grave marker lies a young man, Martin Treptow, who left his job in a small town barbershop in 1917 to go to France with the famed Rainbow Division. There, on the western front, he was killed trying to carry a message between battalions under heavy artillery fire.

We're told that on his body was found a diary. On the flyleaf under the heading "My Pledge," he had written these words: "America must win this war. Therefore I will work, I will save, I will sacrifice, I will endure, I will fight cheerfully and do my utmost, as if the issue of the whole struggle depended on me alone."

In 1982, President Reagan again evoked pride and love of country when he closed a radio address with this hospital story:

Not long ago marine commandant P. C. Jones visited the hospital in Lebanon that houses those injured in the recent terrorist attack. One blind marine, swathed from head to toe in bandages, didn't believe it was the top marine general visiting his bedside. He reached up to the general's shoulder and counted the number of stars—one, two, three, four.

The private nodded and then signaled with his two hands for a pad and paper. Then he wrote "Semper Fi" for Semper Fideles. "Always faithful."

Shouldn't we always keep faith with those brave men and women?

Old Soldiers Never Die

I remember being let out of my prep school classes in 1951 to hear the dismissed General MacArthur end his address to the joint session of Congress. Here is his closer:

> The world has turned over many times since I took the oath on the plains at West Point, and the hopes and dreams have long since vanished. But I still remember the refrain of one of the most popular barrack ballads of that day, which proclaimed most proudly that "old soldiers never die; they just fade away."
>
> And like the old soldier of that ballad, I now close my military career and just fade away—an old soldier who tried to do his duty as God gave him the light to see that duty.
>
> Good-bye.

Free at Last

Dr. Martin Luther King preached hope in his "I Have a Dream" speech when he offered inspiration from an old hymn—to lift the listeners to soaring rapture.

> When we let freedom ring, when we let it ring from every village and every hamlet, from every state and every city, we will be able to speed up that day when all of God's children, black men and white men, Jews and Gentiles, Protestants and Catholics, will be able to join hands and sing in the words of the old Negro spiritual, "Free at last! Free at last! Thank God Almighty, we are free at last!"

Apply Their Anecdotes

All these titans of speech knew the secrets of making an emotional close. John Kennedy and Ronald Reagan employed historical anecdotes. Churchill drew from the Bible and poetry. Douglas MacArthur and Martin Luther King closed with lyrics from a ballad or hymn.

And you can borrow the stories they once used. I heard a business leader who was cutting a ribbon for a new bank branch close with the Franklin story about the chair at the constitutional convention. After he quoted Franklin's "a new day for America and a new dawn for freedom," he added this:

> Well, this new branch represents a new day for and new horizons for Williamsport.

Another executive closed a pep talk to his employees with the marine hospital story Reagan told, adding his own final line:

> And so let us keep faith with the ideals of our company's founder: Service is our signature of quality.

Some executives have said to me, "But Jamie, I give few talks." Wrong! You deliver a talk every time you introduce a speaker for the civic club or make an in-house presentation. You talk every time you give out an employee-of-the-month award or a retirement gift. You talk every time you make a presentation to another company or when you speak at a conference table in a company planning session. And every time you open your mouth, your capability as a leader is judged.

EVERY TIME YOU OPEN YOUR MOUTH, YOUR CAPABILITY AS A LEADER IS JUDGED.

When the close of your presentation or pitch falls flat, your prospects for advancement fizzle.

Let's imagine you are asked to make a presentation to an employee. You might want to cite this story about Winston Churchill:

> In 1940, Churchill was signing the Victoria Cross to a member of the Home Guard who had rescued five lives under a burning building that had been destroyed in the blitz. The man said, "Mr. Churchill, you honor me."
>
> Churchill replied, "Ah, but you are wrong! You are the one who honors me."

Another effective finale I heard was given by a CEO who saluted a retiring employee with this story from Scripture:

> When I think of our honoree, Alvin, I think of Solomon in the Bible when the angel of the Lord visited him and asked him what he needed most to be king: "Riches? Power? or Fame?"
>
> Solomon answered, "Give me an understanding heart."
>
> Well, when you listen to these stories from some of his co-workers on the contributions and random kindnesses he has performed, we know that God gave Alvin an understanding heart.

Draw from History

Historical anecdotes also make good endings. Winston Churchill's great-great-grandfather, Reuben Murray, was a lieutenant in the Continental Army under General Washington. When an associate raised the problem of a western front, Churchill ended his cabinet meeting with this anecdote:

> General George Washington had a general on his staff known as "Mad Anthony" Wayne, who told him: "I'll storm hell, General Washington, if you'll only plan the assault."
>
> And Washington replied, "Perhaps, my dear General Wayne, we should try Stony Point first in the Hudson River!"
>
> And so, let's first concentrate on North Africa before talking about a western front.

Create a Cathedral

Ronald Reagan was a spokesman for General Electric before he ran for Governor of California in 1966. He would offer up this story in pep talks to General Electric employees across America.

> During the Middle Ages, three stone masons were observed at the city of Cologne in Germany doing their work. The onlooker asked the first what he was doing. He looked up and answered, "I am shaping stone." The next mason was asked the same question and he replied, "I am making a wall." But when the third mason was given the question, he proclaimed proudly, "I am creating a cathedral."
>
> And you are here creating a cathedral of energy.

Adopt the closing style of two of the greatest communicators and motivators in history: Reagan and Churchill.

Plus Ultra

Or you can lift historical closes told by the second greatest British prime minister in the past century, Margaret Thatcher.

In a visit to a Texas software company, she talked about the discoveries being made in technology by American business. She closed with this:

> When Christopher Columbus set sail in 1492, his flagship, the *Santa Maria,* carried the flag of Queen Isabella of Castille, which bore a representation of a castle with the words *Ne plus Ultra*— "nothing further"—under it because Spain was considered the farthest point west in the world.
>
> When Columbus returned and reported his discoveries in the New World to the queen, she ordered a court painter to modify the flag so that it now read *"plus ultra"*—"more beyond" or "more out there."
>
> Well, with new technology and more opportunities—there is more out there.

My Favorite Three

Three of my favorite closers that I suggest to executives are stories involving General Eisenhower.

The first piece of land General Eisenhower ever owned was the farm he bought in Gettysburg after World War II. When he was asked by the recording clerk in the Gettysburg county courthouse at the time of the settlement why he wanted to have that property, he replied, "All my life I have lived on an army post, but when I die, I want to leave a piece of earth and leave it to God better than I found it."

> **ADOPT THE CLOSING STYLE OF TWO OF THE GREATEST COMMUNICATORS AND MOTIVATORS IN HISTORY: REAGAN AND CHURCHILL.**

Here's the second:

In the spring of 1945, at dawn, as the Allied armies were about to cross the Rhine River in Germany, a G.I. was restlessly pacing by the riverbank.

"What's the matter, soldier?" asked an observer as he approached.

The young man replied, "I guess I'm a little nervous."

"Well, so am I," said the other; "let us walk together by the river and perhaps we'll draw strength from each other."

The private did not know that the arm around his shoulder was that of General Eisenhower.

And the third:

In March 1969, General Eisenhower was dying at Walter Reed Hospital. One evening he called his son John, who was in a suite on the floor below him.

When John Eisenhower entered the room, he found his father lying in an oxygen tent. "Pull me up, Johnny," he said. "Tell them, John, that I have always loved my wife, I've always loved my children, I've always loved my grandchildren, I've always loved my country, and I have always loved my God."

Pick a Proven Closer

One of the greatest Democratic Party orators in the past century was former vice president Hubert Humphrey. A supporter of Humphrey, a mogul in the film industry, lifted this closing that he had once heard Humphrey deliver.

> When Franklin Roosevelt died in Warm Springs, Georgia, in April of 1945, he was posing for a portrait and was composing a speech for the Jefferson/Jackson Day dinner.
>
> The president suddenly slumped over. The last words he wrote were: "The only limit to our realization of tomorrow is our doubts of today."

Imagine the emotional impact of closing with the last words of one of our greatest presidents! But your closer doesn't have to be a tearjerker. Any powerful ending will serve the purpose for ending an introduction, an award ceremony, or a proposal in a board meeting.

It Is People Who Count

An executive noted that her fellow Wellesley alumna, Cokie Roberts of ABC, had once used this close in her introduction of a speaker:

> Some years ago Alice Freeman Palmer, then president of Wellesley College, was told by her husband that she should retire and devote herself to writing. She rejected his advice by saying: "It is people that count—you put yourself in people, they touch other people; these, others still, and so you go on working forever."
>
> And our speaker today is a splendid example of one who puts herself in people.

Plant a Flower

President Ford once honored a humanitarian who had been active in the National Conference of Christians and Jews. He ended his tribute with this anecdote:

Whenever the better angels of our nature are appealed to, we think of the man who first coined that phrase, President Abraham Lincoln. Let us also think of the epitaph he once said he wanted on his tombstone; it applies to our honoree today.

"When I die, I want it said of me that I always plucked a thistle and planted a flower where I thought a flower would grow."

You might appropriate that ending for that selfless, giving employee or civic volunteer you may introduce or present an award to in the future.

Three-Handkerchief Special

If you want an ending that will guarantee a standing ovation, try this "three-handkerchief special" with which Jack Kemp once closed a Memorial Day address. In your case, the occasion might be one honoring the deceased founder of a company or a departed town leader.

One of the greatest football coaches was Lou Little of Columbia University. General Eisenhower, who was president of the university after the war, included him as one of the greatest leaders he ever knew. Before Little was at Columbia, he was coach at Georgetown. In 1928, he had a reserve end named Dennis Flaherty who came into scrimmage every afternoon with an older man.

On the day of their game with their big rival, Holy Cross, Flaherty asked, "Mr. Little, may I start in today's game?"

"Son," replied Little, "you're too small—I know you give your heart out in scrimmage. That's why I sometimes put you in at the end of the game when it doesn't matter."

"Well, Mr. Little, I've prayed. If I don't do everything an end should do, pull me out after the first five minutes."

Well, Coach Little let Flaherty start, and Flaherty played all sixty minutes that day. Flaherty blocked a kick, sacked the quarterback twice, intercepted one pass, and caught another for a touchdown. After the game Little said, "Flaherty, how did you know you could even play such a game?"

"Well, Mr. Little, that was my dad I came with every day."

"I gathered that," said Little.

"Well, Dad was blind," explained Flaherty, "and last night he died of a heart attack. And so you see, Coach Little, today was the first time Dad would ever see me play."

To that you can add, "Well I sense our Founder is looking down at us . . ."

You can call on the anecdote closer for delivering an incisive point as well as an inspiring plea.

A Philadelphia insurance executive who is a Civil War buff once closed a staff meeting with this ending:

> In the Civil War Admiral David Farragut called Captain Samuel DuPont into his office to account for his failure to take his gunboats into Charleston Harbor. Captain DuPont listed five reasons why he didn't make the raid.
>
> Farragut replied, "Captain, there was another reason that you have not mentioned."
>
> "What is that?"
>
> "You did not believe you could do it."

Imagine Your Obituary

Some day you may need a powerful closer at a fundraiser. To be prepared, you may want to store in your file this one by Ambassador Adlai Stevenson:

> The close of the nineteenth century found a Swedish businessman settling down to his breakfast of kippers, eggs, and bacon. As he sipped his morning coffee, he glanced at the *Stockholm Journal*.
>
> To his astonishment, he found his picture emblazoned on the front page. He read further. It was an obituary!
>
> He knew at once that they had confused him with his brother, who had just died in the East Indies, but he had to read what they wrote about him. To his chagrin, he found phrases such as "Merchant of Munitions," "Dealer of Destruction," "Peddler of Death" applied to him.

Immediately he called for his carriage to take him to his solicitor's office. There he wrote a new will—a will that established the Nobel Peace Foundation.

You Are His Hands

Note another powerful closer, this one by Governor Mario Cuomo:

> In a little town in Southern Italy the statue of Christ was shattered by the German artillery as they left the town in 1944. The priest told the men to search for the arms, legs, and head and then assemble the pieces while the womenfolk prepared a village feast.
>
> But at dusk the townsmen came to the priest in despair. "Padre, we have tried to put it back together—but there are no hands for Jesus. They are shattered into bits."
>
> "Children," the priest replied, "don't you realize? *You* are His hands."

Find Your Own Ending

Some of the best endings may come from your own experience. The CEO of a pet products company was feeling a challenge by some of the big national companies. I was a consultant asked to draft a talk for his employees and sales force around the country. When I asked him for any emotional experiences in his life, he said, "No."

> SOME OF THE BEST ENDINGS MAY COME FROM YOUR OWN EXPERIENCE.

I pressed: "That's amazing. No grandparents died? No parents died?"

He answered, "Actually, when I was at college my father died. I went back home and helped Mom with the arrangements. Then two weeks later Mom died. This time I did all the arrangements by myself—the funeral, the minister, picking out the dress for the service, the cemetery, and the interment rites. When I got back from the cemetery, I opened the door and there was Rex, our Labrador, dead at the bottom of the stairs."

So, I had him close his talk with that story, with this addition: "I didn't give up then, and I'm not giving up now. We're going to come back stronger than ever."

This was a dog lovers' group. They had all bought his fencing product for their own dogs. I watched the videotape of his talk. There wasn't a dry eye in the audience.

Crisp Closers—Electric Endings

So mine your own memories for that poignant experience. The difference between polite and hearty applause depends most on how you finish your talk.

> THE DIFFERENCE BETWEEN POLITE AND HEARTY APPLAUSE DEPENDS MOST ON HOW YOU FINISH YOUR TALK.

"Crisp closers," "electric endings," and, yes, "terminal tearjerkers" are devices to give force to that finish. This chapter offers you "fingertip finales" for almost any talk.

No matter if your speech is a bit banal and blah, you can still close in a blaze of glory. The last impression is the one most indelibly etched in memory. A dull speech that ends in a dazzle gets more applause than a forceful speech that ends on a flat note.

> "CRISP CLOSERS," "ELECTRIC ENDINGS," AND, YES, "TERMINAL TEARJERKERS" ARE DEVICES TO GIVE FORCE TO THAT FINISH.

So keep in mind that if you are preparing a presentation that sounds a little pedestrian, you can still trigger a big hand by giving an emotional finale.

Copy Kennedy and King and other greats from history, or adapt one of your own anecdotes to wind up your talk with a Power Close that triggers a standing ovation.

21

Power Audacity

Arm me with audacity.

—William Shakespeare

Dare to be different! That's what made Churchill, Reagan, and Lincoln tower above the crowd. Leaders don't play it safe. Leaders don't always follow the script. They do the unexpected. They pull surprises. They catch their audience unawares. They make moves that live in the memories of their listeners.

Surprise Your Audience

What did Reagan do when he met Premier Gorbachev at Berlin for the 1986 conference? Did he observe the usual niceties of negotiation? Did he follow the traditional dictates of diplomacy? Was his speech the customary Foggy Bottom bureaucratese? No, he was blunt:

> Mr. Gorbachev, tear down that wall!

Reagan knew that what the situation called for was not some bland cant of banalities but words that would move and shape history.

Benjamin Franklin practiced the art of surprise, as this story demonstrates:

Early in Benjamin Franklin's career, the proprietors of Philadelphia tried to drive the uppity printer out of the city by cutting him out of all government contracts and legal documents in both city and province.

> **COMMUNICATION IS MORE THAN JUST THE WORDS YOU EXPRESS. IT IS ALSO THE IMPRESSION YOU MAKE.**

Franklin decided to send out engraved invitations to the proprietors to come to his house. Out of curiosity, they came.

Did Franklin then serve up a fattened pig for a feast to be washed down by good French wine to win over the proprietors? No. Before each guest Franklin had set a bowl of something that looked like gray mush. Franklin, at the head of the table, took a pitcher of water, added some to his bowl, and then proceeded to wolf down the contents greedily.

One of his guests then poured some water into his bowl and tried a spoonful. He spat it out quickly, saying, "Good heavens, Franklin, what the devil is in this bowl?"

Franklin smilingly replied, "Plain old sawdust. And if you understand that I can live off that, you ought to know you'll never squeeze me out of my business."

Franklin dared to be different and got back on the city government printing list.

What did Richard Nixon do when he was invited to speak at the 1992 Republican convention—the first convention he would have addressed since 1972? He turned down the invitation. Later he told me why:

> **LEADERS DON'T ALWAYS FOLLOW THE SCRIPT. THEY MAKE MOVES THAT LIVE IN THE MEMORIES OF THEIR LISTENERS.**

Jamie, a speech by a former Republican president defending the current president is too predictable. A leader can never be boring.

Speakers can't manifest podium power by doing the predictable and prosaic. That is what those who open with polite amenities do. Banalities are boring.

Most speakers we hear rush right into their talk after being introduced. Leaders, however, wait—and force the silence to dramatize their powerful opening statements.

What did Abraham Lincoln do at Gettysburg? His audience at the cemetery sat through two hours of Edward Everett's oration—and then waited a little longer for the president's address. Lincoln took off his stovepipe hat, fixed his steel-rim spectacles on his nose, and then pulled from his pocket pages of what appeared to be a handwritten manuscript. His listeners settled in for a stately and lengthy discourse.

But Lincoln surprised his audience. He did not read the speech in his hands—in fact, he didn't even look down at it. He focused on his listeners and spoke directly to them as if from his heart—for only *two minutes.*

Stage Your Scene

Leaders such as Churchill, Reagan, and Lincoln knew how to stage a scene. Churchill, for example, did so in 1925 when, as the new chancellor of the exchequer, he estimated incoming revenues during his first presentation of the budget. When he came to the excise tax on liquor, he reached for the carafe on the table and poured himself a glassful. But the tumbler he filled took on the amber color of whiskey; it was clearly not water. Churchill, with an impish smile, said,

> It is imperative to fortify the revenue, and this I shall now—with the permission of the Commons—do.

SPEAKERS CAN'T GAIN PODIUM POWER BY DOING THE PREDICTABLE AND PROSAIC.

His sip of whiskey triggered laughter in the House. Only Churchill could have made a presentation of a budget something other than boring!

Churchill definitely knew how to steal the spotlight, as this episode illustrates:

> Aneurin Bevan, the Socialist firebrand, was in the midst of a lengthy tirade against Prime Minister Churchill. But then the Labourite was disconcerted by the spectacle of Churchill crawling on his knees alongside of the front bench. Bevan stopped and asked what the right honorable member was doing.
>
> Churchill flashed a look of innocence and effectively claimed the audience's attention by saying, "I'm looking for my Jujubes [gumdrops]. They fell on the floor."

General Eisenhower wrote how Churchill—in their weekly Friday dinners at Chequers during World War II—would suddenly burst into Shakespeare soliloquies or sonnets. Once, Ike recalled, Churchill recited the passage from *As You Like It,* "All the world's a stage, and all the men and women merely players . . ."

Churchill, however, preferred starring roles. In World War I, when Germany invaded France through neutral Belgium, the British military command recommended a diversionary operation in Antwerp to keep German troops that were deployed to Belgium away from France. Churchill, donning the uniform of his honorific position as Elder of the Trinity House, commandeered five red Piccadilly buses and landed in Antwerp with two thousand untested Royal Marines.

IT WAS ACTOR REAGAN WHO TURNED THE STATE OF THE UNION ADDRESS FROM A DRY LITANY OF RECOMMENDED BILLS INTO A MEMORABLE PAGEANT.

In his gold-braided eighteenth-century uniform and purple tricornered hat, Churchill looked like a cross between a circus ringmaster and Napoleon. But the grandiose spectacle of Churchill atop one of the buses barking orders into a megaphone as he directed the setting up of the defensive positions caught the German Imperial Command's attention and forced the Germans to divert battalions to Antwerp from the French front.

Ronald Reagan, of course, was an actor by profession. Remember how he derailed the Bush momentum in the 1980 New Hampshire primary?

> The Reagan committee had rented a hall in Manchester for a debate between the GOP contenders—Bush, John Anderson, Howard Baker, and Jack Kemp as well as Reagan. The moderator, Mr. Breen, set up a format that allocated time for questions and responses. At one point Breen cut off Reagan in mid-answer. Reagan heatedly said, "I paid for this microphone, Mr. Green [*sic*]."

It was actor Reagan who turned the State of the Union Address from a dry litany of recommended bills into a memorable pageant. Reagan introduced "the man in the audience" ploy, using it for the first time in February 1983, just after a Delta Airliner with icy wings crashed into the Potomac. To Congress and the television audience, Reagan recounted the heroics of a Daniel Stoltnik, who dove into the frigid river to pull out a survivor. Then he pointed to Stoltnik in the gallery, who was seated next to Nancy Reagan.

No one connects Lincoln to the theater—except as the morbid site of his assassination—yet Lincoln kept a copy of *Shakespeare's Tragedies* on his executive mansion desk alongside the Constitution and the King James Version of the Bible. Lincoln, like Churchill, was fond of reciting passages from *Macbeth, Hamlet,* and *King Lear.*

Lincoln understood the dramatics of the unexpected move. He was not afraid to risk dignity to prove a point, as he did in this case:

> Lincoln, representing a man accused of assault and battery, argued that his client had acted in self-defense. Lincoln told the jury that his client, while walking along the highway with a pitch-

fork over his shoulder, was attacked by a fierce dog that ran out at him from a farmer's yard. The man warded off the beast with his pitchfork and one of its prongs pierced and killed the dog.

In his summary to the jury, Lincoln recounted the exchange between the two men:

"What made you kill my dog?" said the dog's owner.

"What made him bite me?" replied the man with the pitchfork.

"But why did you not go after him with the other end of the pitchfork?" asked the dead dog's master.

Lincoln's client answered, "And why did he not come at me with his other end?"

At this Mr. Lincoln got down on his knees, whirled, and pushed his rear end toward the jury box as its members laughed.

An acquittal was the result.

To communicate a point, Lincoln and Churchill would, if the situation demanded it, literally crawl on their knees. They were unafraid of risking their image. They dared to be different in their approach.

Dare to Be Different

I've learned from these masters that one can gain a great deal by taking the risk of doing the unexpected. During the presidential campaign of 1968, I was invited to speak on behalf of Richard Nixon to the followers of Father Divine outside Philadelphia. Even though the black founder of the sect had died in 1965, the movement of thousands still flourished across the country. I arrived in the company of two Nixon campaign aides who had given me a text to read—of the "Black Capitalism" speech written by Nixon. The meeting followed a feast in a huge church hall. In the front were two thrones—the larger one empty, the smaller one occupied by Mother Divine, the handsome white widow of the charismatic cleric.

> ONE CAN GAIN A GREAT DEAL BY TAKING THE RISK OF DOING THE UNEXPECTED.

Out from the empty throne came a booming voice: "Children, you cannot see me but I can see you. . . ." Then came a short inspirational sermon in Father Divine's booming voice, followed by a chorus of "Hallelujah"s and "Amen, Father Divine"s that had obviously been taped years earlier.

I had sensed from the patriotic hymns before his message and by the content of Father Divine's sermon that the speech I'd been given would not work. I instead addressed the empty throne:

> It is an honor to be in your spiritual presence, Father Divine, and to be lifted by your message. As you and Mother Divine know, the Pilgrims landed in 1620 saying, "In the name of God, Amen!" And we recall how Thomas Jefferson wrote in the Declaration of Independence: "endowed by our Creator." Then we remember how Benjamin Franklin implored the Constitutional convention: "If no sparrow can fall far from the heavens without His notice, surely no nation can be built without His help." And we should note how Abraham Lincoln, a few days before he went to Ford's Theater on that fateful evening, issued a proclamation that put "In God We Trust" on the nickel.
>
> When I served as a Pennsylvania legislator, I used to look at the mural behind the Speaker's rostrum. It displayed a sheriff—John Nixon—reading the Declaration of Independence from the tower atop what is now called Independence Hall. Sheriff Nixon had been warned that it was too revolutionary a document to read publicly, but Nixon had replied that engraved on the bell in the tower were these words from Leviticus: "Proclaim freedom to all of the world and all the inhabitants thereof."
>
> "I'm not afraid," said Sheriff Nixon, "to proclaim freedom to the world."
>
> And so I ask you, Father Divine, to let Sheriff John Nixon's collateral descendant, Richard Nixon, proclaim freedom to all the world.

After resounding "Amen"s and "Hallelujah"s, Mother Divine prayed to ask guidance from Father Divine. After some silence she told the assembled congregation, "Father Divine has endorsed Richard Nixon and asks you to give your votes and your dollars to his cause."

The next day the *Philadelphia Tribune,* the black newspaper, was headlined: "FATHER DIVINE ENDORSES NIXON."

I dared to be different—and succeeded.

Depart from Convention to Gain Attention

Years later, Reagan got the nation's attention when he chose to be different. For decades the State of the Union Address was a tedious recital of programs to be advanced. Reagan knew that, because of television, his audience was more the American people than the legislators in the Capitol chamber.

If Reagan could sell the people, Congress would have to follow. So he dared to be different. He delivered an uplifting talk with one theme—featuring limited government or the export of freedom. The specific bills followed later.

Actually the modern format, in which the State of the Union Address is delivered by the president to a joint session of Congress, was re-introduced by President Woodrow Wilson. Presidents Washington and Adams delivered the annual message in person to the House and Senate, but Jefferson had his message sent over, and his successors followed the practice. Wilson, who had a doctorate in political science, had once written a treatise called *Parliamentary Government.* During his study of British institutions, he became intrigued with the custom of the British monarch delivering an annual address (written by the prime minister) to the House of Commons.

The daily newspaper in the emerging twentieth century had become a powerful force in shaping public opinion, and Wilson wanted to seize its front page by presenting his message personally to Congress. Wilson dared to be different.

His predecessor, Theodore Roosevelt, dared to be different when he inaugurated the press conference in the White House. By doing so, Teddy became the pet of the press, just as the teddy bear, which took its name from the president, became the country's most popular toy.

In 1912, when Theodore Roosevelt was running for president on the Progressive Party ticket, he would shock his audience by speaking after he was shot in the chest by a would-be assassin while en route from his hotel in Milwaukee. Although the bullet tore through his chest and his coat was covered with blood, he began:

Friends, I shall ask you to be very quiet and please excuse me from making a very long speech. I'll do the best I can, but you see, there's a bullet in my body.

He spoke for fifty minutes and then went to the hospital.

Theodore Roosevelt was a showman. He knew the fact that he made the speech would be more important than the speech itself. He dared to be different.

In another dramatic way, if not so dangerous, his distant cousin Franklin Roosevelt dared to be different in 1932. He chartered a ten-passenger trimotor plane in July of that year to fly to deliver his acceptance speech at the Democratic convention—a historical "first" and a dramatic move. Roosevelt communicated that he was the right man for the job—a decisive leader in a time of economic crisis. His precedent-breaking flight captured more attention than did his actual speech. Dare to be different!

Another luminary, Fiorello La Guardia, one of New York's greatest mayors, dared to be different—whether he was reading the "funnies" over the radio during a newspaper strike or riding on the back of a fire engine to a fire. The following anecdote captures an event that occurred while the mayor was presiding at police court:

On that cold day they brought a trembling old man before him, charged with stealing a loaf of bread. His family, he said, was starving.

"I've got to punish you," declared La Guardia. "The law makes no exception. I can do nothing but sentence you to a fine of ten dollars."

But La Guardia, also known as the "Little Flower," was already reaching into his pocket as he added: "Well, here's the ten dollars to pay for your fine. And now I remit the fine." He then tossed a ten-dollar bill into his famous sombrero!

"Furthermore," La Guardia declared, "I'm going to fine everybody in this courtroom fifty cents for living in a town where a man has to steal bread in order to eat. Mr. Bailiff, collect the fines and give them to this defendant!"

The hat was passed and the incredulous old man, with a light of heaven in his eyes, left the courtroom with a stake of forty-seven dollars and fifty cents.

Be Bold

It often takes a certain flair to dare to be different, to break precedent, to stray from the script, to do the unexpected. By doing the unexpected, you might also bail yourself out of an awkward situation, as Eisenhower once did. During World War II, before D day, General Eisenhower delivered hundreds of "morale" speeches while inspecting troops. The best he ever gave was in Plymouth in early April 1944. There, on the tarmac, the troops stood at attention awaiting the supreme Allied commander. As he approached the assembled soldiers, he slipped on the wet surface, sodden from spring rains. He took a flip and landed on his backside in the mud. The troops stood mute as Eisenhower picked himself up and brushed off his uniform. Then, looking at the men, he let loose a huge guffaw. It triggered gales of laughter from the men. Eisenhower then raised his two arms in a "vee" salute and walked off.

Ike later commented: "It was the best speech I ever gave."

An unconditional display of courage can send an unusually strong message. When the Japanese surrendered in 1945, General MacArthur flew to Japan, landing at Narita Airport, which is close to thirty miles from the center of the metropolis. An armored car had been selected as his conveyance into the city. MacArthur chose instead an open limousine. Staff members who were traveling with him inspected their rifles and pistols, but MacArthur said, "No firearms."

> AN UNCONDITIONAL DISPLAY OF COURAGE CAN SEND AN UNUSUALLY STRONG MESSAGE.

Then the slow drive into Tokyo commenced. MacArthur stood in the back of the open car, arms raised high as he passed by hundreds of thousands of Japanese troops lining the road, all standing at attention. The Japanese were awed by this display of courage. MacArthur dared to be different.

Be bold. Act audaciously. Dare to be different.

Index